THE ROAR
ON THE OTHER SIDE

Also by the author:

Sketches of Home

What a Light Thing, This Stone

The Weather of the House

A Welcome Shore

THE ROAR ON THE OTHER SIDE

A GUIDE FOR STUDENT POETS

SUZANNE U. RHODES

Published by Canon Press
P.O. Box 8729, Moscow, ID 83843
800.488.2034 | www.canonpress.com

Suzanne U. Rhodes, *The Roar on the Other Side: A Guide for Student Poets*

Revised edition, 2009.

Cover design by Rachel Hoffmann.
Interior design by Laura Storm.

Printed in the United States of America.

Library of Congress Cataloging-in-Publication Data

Rhodes, Suzanne U.
The roar on the other side : a guide for student poets / Suzanne U. Rhodes. -- Rev. ed.
p. cm.
Includes indexes.
ISBN-13: 978-1-885767-66-0 (pbk.)
ISBN-10: 1-885767-66-8 (pbk.)
1. English language--Rhetoric. 2. Poetry--Authorship--Problems, exercises, etc. 3. Creative writing--Problems, exercises, etc. I. Title.
PE1408.C5217 2009
808.1--dc22

2008053382

22 23 24 25 9 8 7 6 5 4

FOR
LESLIE

“In every poem there is some
of the substance of God.”
—St. Augustine

Contents

Introduction

Poetry starts with silence—not silence in the world but silence of mind.

To write you must learn quiet. This is hard, because the world we live in is loud. There is the noise of TV, traffic, sirens, telephones, dishwashers, barking dogs, lawn mowers. You get in a car and the radio is automatically blaring. At the mall, you shop to the stampede of rock. "We will make the whole universe a noise," boasted Screwtape in C. S. Lewis's classic work, *The Screwtape Letters*. "The melodies and silences of Heaven will be shouted down in the end."

Our Creator asks us to "Be still and know that I am God." Not many people practice being still. Even young children today seem to have sprouted headphones. If we cultivate the art of inner quiet and develop habits to nurture the mind's green fields, we will hear the melodies of Heaven.

Noise, of course, is not a bad thing. Loud noise is thrilling: sirens, fireworks, band music, semi-trucks, thunder, stadium cheers, avalanches. But stillness needs a larger room than most of us give it. By making decisions to read a good book instead of watching TV or take a walk instead of playing a video game, you are enlarging this room. Writing poetry will add floor space and a skylight.

God made our minds to love Him. We do this by first coming to the cross of Christ for salvation, where, as the hymn says, "sinners plunged beneath that flood lose all their guilty stains." We love God with our minds by being renewed through His Word and thinking about excellent, lovely, wholesome things. Did you know that when you study birds (ornithology), bugs (entomology), words (etymology), the human body (anatomy), and just about any "-ology" you can think of, you are loving Him? "The works of the Lord are great, studied by all who have pleasure in them," wrote the psalmist. We love God with our mind when we admire smoothness, strangeness, structure, intricacy, fragrance, complexion, motion. "Glory be to God for dappled things," exclaimed the poet-priest Gerard Manley Hopkins.

So then, noticing what God has made is important. In noticing, we name. Thus Adam became the first poet. He named every striped, spotted, winged, webbed, slow, swift creature. He was creative. When you think of words to perfectly name what you feel and see and hear, you are also creating. Noticing and naming are the subjects of chapters one and two.

Using metaphors, similes, and other figures of speech (language that can't be taken literally) adds even more delight, as when Emily Dickinson describes a sunrise: "I'll tell you how the sun rose/A ribbon at a time./The steeples swam in amethyst/The news like squirrels ran." In chapter three, you'll learn about metaphorming, the art of seeing similarities.

Here's how Daniel Marion, a prominent poet from Tennessee, describes his favorite barbecue place:

Song for Wood's Barbeque Shack in McKenzie, Tennessee

Here in mid-winter let us begin
to lift our voices in the pine woods:

O sing praise to the pig
who in the season of first frost
gave his tender hams and succulent shoulders
to our appetite:
praise to the hickory embers
for the sweetest smoke
a man is ever to smell,
its incense a savor
of time bone deep:
praise for Colonel Wood and all his workers
in the dark hours who keep watch
in this turning of the flesh
to the delight of our taste:
praise to the sauce—vinegar, pepper, and tomato—
sprinkled for the tang of second fire:
Praise we say now for mudwallow, hog grunt and
  pig squeal,
snorkle snout ringing bubbles of swill in the trough,
each slurp a sloppy vowel of hunger,
jowl and hock, fatback and sowbelly, root dirt and pure
piggishness of sow, boar, and barrow.

One thing that makes this poem so much fun is the delectable sounds the author selects: "snorkle snout ringing bubbles . . . sloppy vowel of hunger"—take your pick! In this book you will learn about sounds in poetry, and rhythm too. Consider the rhythms of these lines by John Donne: "Batter my heart, three-person'd God; for you/As yet but knock, breathe, shine, and seek to mend." In the poem, God is pictured as a tinker (one who sells and repairs pots and pans) who has to do a lot of pounding and hammering to make the subject of the poem, a sinner, yield to His grace. Notice how the rhythm advances the meaning. We feel the glancing blows through Donne's skillful use of monosyllabic words: knock, breathe, shine, seek. Sound and rhythm are the subjects of chapters four and five.

Chapters six through eight consider such things as sonnets and stanzas, white space and planned freefalls—

what we call form. Chapter nine covers types of poems, or genres; chapter ten, voice and diction. Chapter eleven offers practical advice for reading, writing, and revising poems. It also encourages young writers to seek recognition of their work. We'll discuss manuscript preparation, researching poetry markets and contests, and the nuts and bolts of submitting material.

Finally, the book includes a section called "Gathering of Poems" followed by a series of exercises and writing projects in addition to those included in the text under the heading "Stepping Stones." There is also a glossary of literary terms.

To use this book successfully, you'll need some basic equipment. Most important is the journal. Buy an attractive, bound book with lined paper. The ideal size is 8½ by 11 inches, but a midsized one will do. All of your writing will go in this journal: lists, word-play, free-writing, and other activities and exercises assigned in the book. Don't worry about neatness and perfect sentences. A typical free-writing entry may simply be a series of phrases, as in this passage I wrote in response to the word shower: *Rain and melting hair streams and storms, quick tattoos and drenching rinsing nailing singing water.*

The other equipment you'll need is a computer or typewriter and a colored folder with pockets to keep your poems in. All poems should be typed. Plan on revising your poems many times, for the writing process is one of re-vising, which means "re-seeing." See what words need to be cut, what images added, what lines rearranged. At the end of the course, you will want to choose some to send to contests and magazines that publish poetry written by young people. As I said earlier, it is important to seek audiences. Just as words are a gift from God, I believe the skillful poet has gifts for readers. Thinking about publishing your writing helps you develop and improve. Even rejection slips—inevitable and so disheartening—play a role in toughening and training.

Finally, because all writers are apprentices, it is important to study the masters, past and present: Shakespeare, Dante, Dickinson, Dillard, Frost. Contemporary poetry is a mixed bag, so be sure to seek parental guidance in your selections. Generous helpings of sumptuous poetry by masters are included throughout the book with hopes you will pursue these authors and read their works in entirety. One thing this book does not do is evaluate poems in terms of the underlying worldview. Other books explore that dimension. I have also included writings of my own gifted students, gathered over the years.

And now, to the fields . . .

1. Sight Training

At the beach one summer, my family and I came across a most curious young man making his way along the shore, a sun-bronzed, wind-blown man with bulging pockets. We greeted him and asked what he was collecting. He sputtered some sounds, then opened his mouth and began removing what looked like small black stones from his inner cheeks.

Once he could speak, he told us he was collecting fossils, that the beach was full of them. I said I had tried to find sharks' teeth for years but never once had spotted one. He began to point out various types of fossils he had collected: bat ray plates, sharks' teeth, vertebrae. I was astounded. He took us to his car, opened the trunk, and showed off his sea horde. "Here's what you look for," he said. "The fossils are shiny black, blacker than any other object on the beach. And they won't break, as shells will."

Since then, I have sat myself down beside many a shell-studded sand mound and plucked out sharks' teeth by the dozens. The young man had taught me how to see. Henry James, the American novelist, gave advice worth following: "Try to be one of the people on whom nothing is lost." A well-trained eye sees the world in particulars. I've learned to spot squawroot, kestrels, and, in deference to my son, Dodge Vipers. (But I still haven't found any arrowheads.)

You are learning to write poetry. You must learn to see.

Stepping Stones

Orange You Glad

» Go to the grocery store with your mind in a canvas state ready for paint. Bring your journal along. Visit the produce section and note names, colors, shapes, textures of vegetables and fruits. When you get home, catalogue in your journal everything you saw. Then choose five or six items that caught your eye and record what you thought and felt in the presence of bananas, kiwis, lettuce, onions, plums, etc. Include details that appeal to the senses.

Please look with me at an orange I'm about to peel.

> It's big as a softball, with thick, bright, fake-looking skin. I dig in my thumbnail like a spade and begin to loosen and tear the hide, exposing a white webbing, a kind of packing material. A tang fine as seaspray scents the air. The globe is seamed and perfectly sectioned. I break the threads to release each segment, fat as a wineskin, and slide one into my mouth. The juice was bottled in Heaven, I am certain. As I eat, it drips from my fingers and lips, lavish and miraculous, until I eat it all, leaving a film of sweetness like gold leaf on my face.

It should be obvious this passage does more than mechanically describe an orange or the act of eating an orange. What else is intended? Write a paragraph discussing the words and the meanings arising from them.

Now you choose a piece of fruit to eat (not an orange). Write a journal entry of your own, describing the experience. Use sensory details and words full of suggestion.

Nature Sleuth

» Buy or check out from the library a field guide to rocks, birds, fossils, moths, pond animals, wildflowers—

whatever interests you in God's wide world so you can name it. For instance, you could identify the various trees in your backyard by consulting the Audubon field guide with its lovely full-color photographs.

Consider yourself a sleuth solving a puzzle. The clues are details that help you classify your object—in the case of a tree: bark, leaves, height, flowers. Record the date, a written description, and a drawing. Use the field guide to help you label your discoveries. If you want to confirm the accuracy of your identification, make an appointment to visit a professor at a local college who is an expert in your subject area. Take your specimens and journal to show him.

Write down freely all the thoughts and feelings that come to you as you examine your specimen. You might consider the object in its natural setting. Don't worry about writing complete sentences or having a topic sentence. Let impressions flow in words, phrases, fragments, sentences, lines of a poem. Follow the trail.

Here's an example:

Holly Tree

Leaves scratch on glass trying to get in. Shiny and sharp as cat claws. Berries like drops of blood. Tree attracts cedar waxwings who arrive yearly on a fixed April day to devour the berries left over from Christmas. Their constant diving and swooping knocks off the old, yellowing leaves to make way for new. In winter, the tree leans with heavy snow but never breaks. It is part of the house, sturdy survivor. An evergreen feast for birds and eyes.

There is more to seeing than observing details, which is what scientists do to gather information. They look to see what is there in order to make factual statements or predictions. But the poet's lens is more like a prism than a telescope; more like a kaleidoscope than a microscope. For the poet takes bare fact and clothes it with meaning. The poet hears the roar on the other side of silence. The poet sees the world in a grain of sand, men as trees walking, and the ocean as a whale-road.[1] He sees with feeling and finds words for his wonder or rage. Blinded by traitors and exiled from home, old Gloucester in Shakespeare's *King Lear* says, "I see it [the world] feelingly."

Poets choose words that are rich in CONNOTATION, a term that refers to emotional associations of language. (DENOTATION is the literal, dictionary meaning of a word.) Another way to say this is that some words are resonant, vibrating like musical sound and carrying meanings that go beyond the literal. To call a dandelion a weed is to condemn it. But a wildflower—now that's a thing of beauty. Jungle or rainforest, wetland or swamp: it's all a matter of perspective. A house in need of repair is a dump and an eyesore to people in the neighborhood, but to the realtor running an ad in the paper, it's "a bargain, a real fixer-upper."

In his poem "The Chimney Sweeper," William Blake wanted to protest the cruel treatment suffered by young boys in the eighteenth century who were sometimes sold for labor by their impoverished parents. The speaker of the poem is a lad who was sold at a young age to a master sweeper. He tries to comfort the newest recruit, a child named Tom Dacre:

> There's little Tom Dacre, who cried when his head,
> That curled like a lamb's back, was shaved; so I said,
> "Hush, Tom! never mind it, for, when your head's bare,
> You know that the soot cannot spoil your white hair."

The second line with its reference to a lamb's back offers a good example of connotation. What is suggested by *lamb*? If you have a baby brother or sister, you know how soft and fine is the hair that curls at the nape of the neck. The tenderness and innocence of a very young child is implied.

[1] These are quotations from a variety of sources, including George Eliot, William Blake, the Bible, and *Beowulf.*

Stepping Stones

Word Vibes

» Write down the different connotations of the words in each group.

- charger Clydesdale nag
- fat obese voluptuous pleasingly plump
- genius nerd bookish
- city slicker ghetto rat homeless person

» Now think of words with different shades of meaning to go with the nouns below:

- country boy
- dog
- homely
- unusual

How to See

» Find a copy of Annie Dillard's book, *A Pilgrim at Tinker Creek*. Read the chapter called "Sight" and write an essay identifying the different ways of seeing she describes.

2. Real Toads

In the forty-ninth chapter of Genesis, we meet a first-rate poet by the name of Naphtali. Father Jacob, an old man with failing eyes, gathers his boys to bless them. To one he says, "Naphtali is a deer let loose. He uses beautiful words."

There is much to be said about this verse. For starters, consider the blessing of being a writer—God's own hand on your head! Second, the word Naphtali means "my wrestling," for Rachel went to great lengths to have this son, as we see in Genesis 30.

Perhaps you picture the poet as one who sits beneath the spreading branches of an old oak tree, who drinks tea with elderly aunts and writes of pastel sunsets and kittens. Well, your picture lies! The poet is more like Hulk Hogan, for his mental muscles are mighty and his concentration unsurpassed. The writer passionately pursues words to give form to blind feeling, but the words hide, tease, play dead. Sometimes there is victory. Grunting and sweating, the poet wrestles words to the page, locks them in a leghold, keeps them down for the count, then comes up in triumph.

Naphtali is called a deer, a deer let loose. What is more graceful, more elusive than a deer bounding over hills, bowing over streams? To write is to let go. Christ has set us free. There are, of course, boundaries, which exist as holy truth. To write a poem that approves a racist point of view or blasphemes God degrades and defiles the creative act.

Anything is possible on the road of fancy. Blue pomegranates and talking stones, living bones and wheels of eyes—all these appear in the Book of Wonders, the Bible. As the Christian philosopher Francis Schaeffer said in his essay *Art and the Bible*, Christ redeems the whole man or woman, including the individual's imagination. But the terrain is not without dangers. There are jackals and lions, two-legged hunters, storms, drought. Writers face temptations great and small: discouragement, pride, laziness, self-pity. We see through a glass darkly, and our knowing is small compared to God's infinite mind. But mostly, you are free.

So there you are, a liberated deer sitting in front of your computer, trying to figure out where on all that vast, glorious white space of the screen to perform your caprioles. Actually, you'd rather be slumped in an easy chair looking at TV. What is there to write?

You start with words, beautiful words, "small shapes in the gorgeous chaos of the world," as poet Diane Ackerman calls them. Where do you get your words? By looking at what's in front of you. The rug, the clock, the rain, the doves. The old tennis shoe with a raggedy past, the smell of burned toast. Everything waits to be recognized.

Here's a sentence from one of my students, eleven-year-old Hannah Lepsch, who looked to see what was there. "In the middle of the table is a large crystal vase where curly willow branches swirl, twist, and dangle wildly over the table and usually over my drawing paper." All I can say is, Wow! The shape of the branches which, though severed and contained, still seem alive because of the power of their wild beauty; the suggestiveness of their dangling over the girl's drawing paper, which reminds us of how creation moves the artist to her own creative act—what luminous, musical thought in one so young.

But you mustn't think *beautiful words* means pretty or precious, like chubby cherub figurines. Beautiful means exact, apt, pleasing. It is beautiful to say, as my daughter Katy did, that bumblebees are "juicy as watermelon," or that a box turtle's neck is "wrinkly as covers" (my son Stephen's words), or that a toad "has pudgy front legs he uses for hands," as our friend Tim Bessell wrote at age eight.

Nor are the subjects of poems necessarily beautiful. "Jenkin seemed to be able to enjoy everything: even ugliness," wrote C. S. Lewis of his friend in *Surprised by Joy.* "I learned from him that we should attempt a total surrender to whatever atmosphere was offering itself at the moment; in a squalid town to seek out those very places where its squalor rose to grimness and almost grandeur, on a dismal day to find the most dismal and dripping wood, on a windy day to seek the windiest ridge."

Beautiful words have interesting sounds with value quite apart from sense: glob, fizzle, rancid, perspicacity. The poet-priest Gerard Manley Hopkins insisted that poetry is "to be heard for its own sake and interest even over and above its interest of meaning." Dylan Thomas said the same thing in his *Poetic Manifesto:*

> I wanted to write poetry in the beginning because I had fallen in love with words. The first poems I knew were nursery rhymes, and before I could read them for myself I had come to love just the words of them, the words alone. What the words stood for . . . was of very secondary importance; what mattered was the sound of them. . . . These words were, to me, as the notes of bells, the sounds of musical instruments, the noises of wind, sea, and rain, the

rattle of milkcarts, the clopping of hooves on cobbles . . . might be to someone, deaf from birth, who has miraculously found his hearing.

Stepping Stones

Grim Grandeur

» Look around town for an ugly site: a vacant, littered lot, a dilapidated building, your basement. In your journal, describe the grimness in such a way that it rises to near-grandeur.

Bric-a-Brac Words

» Comb through the dictionary for words with distinctive sounds. Pay no attention to meaning. Make a list of ten such words. Add a word of your own creation, too (for ideas, read Lewis Carroll's "Jabberwocky"). Now write a poem of 6–12 lines using your words however you please to create a scene. (At this point you may consider meanings for suitability to your purpose. Feel free to add or omit words as needed.) Here are my words and poem: shangrila, seltzer, histrionics, shamble, loquacious, cognac, mesmerize, vitreous, plumage, bric-a-brac.

Cloud shangrilas,
seltzering swamps,
histrionics of summer day:
to shamble and dream in loquacious weeds,
cognac of sun, mesmerized snakes:
to walk under vitreous sky and plumage
of live oaks, bric-a-brac shadows,
cool dream caves.

A poet is a crow. Shiny words, rag and button words catch his eye.

The poet Marianne Moore defined a poem as "Real toads in an imaginary garden." What do you suppose this means?

There is a long Latinate word that is not nearly so charming as real toads. (We'll talk about the imaginary garden in another chapter.) It is the word VERISIMILITUDE. But it is a good word for apprentices because by holding it up to your poem you can see whether or not you are being accurate, which is to say, truthful. The writer Carol Bly said, "Anything we recognize the details of we tend to like a little better."

Verisimilitude means likeness, the appearance of being real. It is the shine on the shoe, the creak of a floor, the rawness of a nose coming in from the cold. It is what the colonial poet Anne Bradstreet *didn't* have when she wrote about the landscape of the New World and made her trees and flowers of English variety. By the way, I am an admirer of Anne Bradstreet. When she writes in her own voice rather than in imitation of poets she had studied, her work is very fine. Writing about a fire that destroyed her house, she shows the trunk and chest and all her "pleasant things" scattered about the lawn (see page 157). This is convincing IMAGERY. By imagery we mean words that evoke the senses: sight, sound, touch, taste, smell. Imagery is to poetry what strings are to a violin or color is to a rainbow.

Have you ever come home from an adventure, burning to tell how you dove from rocks into a deep mountain pool and how later, someone caught a black snake and you got to wear it around your shoulders? Unfortunately your little brother starts talking before you do and steals the story, flattening it by leaving out all the important details. "Guess what? Rob jumped off a cliff into the water and a man found a snake and put it around Rob's shoulders and I got to touch it." End of story. Audience exits.

You would have told it right, building suspense as you described the climb up jagged rocks, then the long look down to the dark pool. And how scared you were but how you jumped anyway, jackknifing into the water that slammed into you like a glacier. It was great! You kept going back, dive after dive, until your skin turned blue. And then some college students that were body surfing in the rapids found a black snake and you got to hold it like a rope of licorice, grasping the neck to keep it from biting. *Real toads,* your story.

Poems and stories aren't summaries. They are the book itself, the movie, the game, the dance. The point is for you to read the words and experience the worlds they make.

In language we find both curtains and windows. Curtains are general, abstract words. "The mountain was majestic." To be a good writer, you must pull back the curtain and look through the window, describing what you see, as Mary Shelley does in *Frankenstein:* "grand shapes . . . congregated round me; the unstained snowy mountaintop, the glittering pinnacle, the pine woods, and ragged, bare ravine, the eagle, soaring amidst the clouds. . . ."

Here is an excerpt from "Birches," a long poem by Robert Frost that wonderfully recreates sounds and sights in the wintry New England woods. The curtains here are wide open:

When I see birches bend to left and right
Across the lines of straighter darker trees,
I like to think some boy's been swinging them
Loaded with ice a sunny winter morning
After a rain. They click upon themselves
As the breeze rises, and turn many-colored
As the stir cracks and crazes their enamel.
Soon the sun's warmth makes them shed crystal shells
Shattering and avalanching on the snow-crust—
Such heaps of broken glass to sweep away
You'd think the inner dome of heaven had fallen.

Aren't these sound-words delicious? Read on.

They are dragged to the withered bracken by the
load,
And they seem not to break; though once they are
bowed
So low for long, they never right themselves:
You may see their trunks arching in the woods
Years afterwards, trailing their leaves on the ground
Like girls on hands and knees that throw their hair
Before them over their heads to dry in the sun.

Read the poem aloud, slowly and deliberately so as to fully hear the sounds. Which words and images do you especially like?

Before you do some writing of your own, let me mention a foundational principle of writing which hopefully you have already learned in school. It is the virtue of conciseness. A skillful writer cuts the fat and thickens the gravy. Cutting the fat means using strong nouns and verbs and omitting excessive adjectives, adverbs, clichés, trite speech, and fillers like "a really pretty girl." Thickening the gravy means choosing words that are richly suggestive: "Death's second self that seals up all in rest."

In poetry, conciseness is taken farther than in prose (sentences and paragraphs). Written in LINES where individual words are highly visible, the language is much compressed. In a poem, "there is really so little room," writes Sylvia Plath. "So little time!" Poems make Plath "think of those round glass Victorian paperweights . . . a clear globe, self-complete, very pure, with a forest or village or family group within it. You turn it upside down, then back. It snows. Everything is changed in a minute. It will never be the same in there—not the fir trees, nor the gables, nor the faces." Another name for this compression is density. Think of density as a loaf of whole-grain bread taken straight from the oven. It is thick and hearty, tasting faintly of molasses. Lines of poems should be like this, full of rich details and meaningful ingredients. How unlike store-bought white bread that can be wadded up into a ball like a piece of paper.

Stepping Stones

Strength Training

» Think of verbs as the muscles of sentences. Replace the weak italicized phrases with strong, effective verbs (you may need to change word order).

1. After a strenuous workout, she *quickly drank* a bottle of water.

2. He spoke to the class in an *extremely loud* voice.

3. The professor *walked slowly* across the campus green.

4. There *were* newspapers all over the table.

5. A turkey vulture *was flying* across the sky.

Let's Chat

» See how many synonyms you can think of for each of the following verbs (use a thesaurus if you run out of ideas).

Example: talk—chat, mutter, converse, whisper, murmur, banter, discuss, argue, blab

eat

run

fall

sleep

laugh

Windows on Words

» Compose sentences based on the phrases below. (Choose four or more.) Pull back the curtains and use imagery to describe what you see, but be concise. Be creative.

Example: the movement of a cat
"A pool of cat slides off the stairs." —Emily Clark, my youngest

1. The sound of a bird in the underbrush
2. The look on his face
3. The movement of a squirrel
4. The way her hair looks
5. The crowd after a game when its team wins
6. An early spring morning
7. Boots on the mat coming in from the snow

Backward Look

» Describe an early childhood memory that involves movement and action.

If verbs are the muscles, nouns are the bones of language. It is important to be *specific* in your writing. The tree is a Douglas fir. The street is Lorcum Lane. The food is steamed rice, chunky stir-fried vegetables, peppermint ice cream.

» Write a poem based on a childhood memory that includes: the name of a neighbor or a street, a color, a sound, and a pair of shoes.

Poetry is "taut truth,"[1] aptly illustrated in a short, untitled poem by an unknown Japanese writer:

Scooping up the moon in the wash basin
and spilling it.

Can you see how much is left unsaid here? Where is the woman who went down to the river to draw water for the

[1] The phrase appears in Lawrence Ferlinghetti's free-verse poem "Constantly risking absurdity" (see page 137).

evening bath? Where is the river? How is it she scoops up the moon? And spills it?

I was walking out of the building where I'd taught a poetry class to children attending a summer arts camp. Desmaine Lewis came up alongside me and said, "I like poetry best [better than acting or painting]. I have a book with a rose in it. The rose looks like it's real, coming out of the book."

Desmaine was not speaking of a photograph or illustration of a rose, but a rose of words. As well as Coleridge or Moore or Shelley, this eight-year-old girl expressed the essence of poetry: a real rose coming out of a book.

3. Metaphors Be With You

I'd like you to go in your yard today and see how many natural objects you can find that remind you of something else. Look at blades of grass, sticks and spiderwebs, honeysuckle, the sky.

Many of the metaphors and similes that appear in my poetry come from where I live—my yard, basement, attic, kitchen. Not very impressive, is it, when you think of Homer and his giants, of Dante and his smoldering, groaning inferno? But Emily Dickinson considered bees and flies, lightning forks and cutlery to be worthy subjects. Zechariah did not despise harness bells, nor Moses breadbowls. I don't know where this quotation came from, but it's one of my favorites: "Truth is so excellent that if it but praises small things, they become noble."

Thus is the turtle worthy, and to say it bumps along like a covered wagon, as Amy Clampitt does, is to make it noble. Telephone lines, in Pat Winship's eyes, are transformed into musical scores with blackbirds for notes. A jellyfish is a parachute, the sun a chariot. Begone with your journal to praise the universe.

On a family trip to Florida, we passed trees draped with Spanish moss. "What does it look like?" I asked Katy. "A lady's shawl," she replied. "Yes, a lady's shawl dripping from the shoulders of trees," I added. On our metaphorical tours, yacht rigging becomes harp strings. Fish fins are seagull feathers. Metaphor involves recognition, the reader's eyes widening as if to say, "It is just so."

SIMILE is a comparison of unlike objects using "like" or "as." Can you identify the humorous simile in this excerpt from John Ciardi's poem "Mummy Slept Late and Daddy Fixed Breakfast"? (The full poem appears on pages 160–161.)

> Daddy fixed breakfast.
> He made us each a waffle.
> It looked like gravel pudding.
> It tasted something awful.

METAPHORS don't use connecting words for comparisons, as in this passage: "When clouds bank, they drop coins of rain" (pun intended!). *Coins of rain* is the metaphor. See if you can spot the two metaphors in this passage from "The Joys of House Wrecking," Larry Richman's poem about demolishing an old house (the full poem appears on pages 159-160):

> I strip away from the sheathing and haul from the attic
> all unretrieved shards, hulks, husks,
> the comic bones of incompetent beds, raggedy rags,
> a gray mattress brain with a low I.Q.

Some metaphors are implied rather than stated: "Hope is the thing with feathers/That perches in the soul" (we infer it's a bird). "Batter my heart" (must be a tinker). One of my favorite implied metaphors appears in *Beowulf,* in the famous underwater battle scene with Grendel's mother. The hero draws "an old sword made by the giants, strong of its edges, glory of warriors" and strikes "angrily so that it bit her hard on the neck, broke the bone-rings." The word *bit* suggests the sword is animal-like in ferocity and strength. Again, it is helpful to remember that with metaphor, we are comparing unlike things. Normally, we don't think of a sword as resembling an animal.

Unlike metaphor, simile ties meaning down. "As a ring of gold in a swine's snout, so is a lovely woman who lacks discretion" (Prov. 11:22). Rocks "at low tide . . . rugg'd with wet seaweed" are as "the back of an old sheepdog or spaniel," to quote Amy Clampitt again. With similes, our delight comes from the containment of seeing only the images given us by the poet and no others: gold ring/indiscreet woman; rocks/backs of dogs. With metaphor, we range farther.

When Jesus proclaims, "I am the Bread of life," He removes all fences of our seeing. He is entirely bread—nourishing, flavorful, essential. Rising and resurrection are in the loaf, too. It is bread enough for the whole world, and of this Bread we must eat or perish. "Unless you eat the flesh of the Son of Man and drink His blood, you have no life in you" (Jn. 6:53). Is this metaphor? Is this not mystery? Let us keep silent.

The ability to make associations between things, what I call METAPHORMING, led the poet and critic I. A. Richards to describe the mind as "a connecting organ." More importantly, it is evidence of God's image in us. How else can we re-see the world as a place where lion and lamb rest side by side, where trees clap their hands, and swords have been beaten into plowshares? How was it Jesus could envision joy surging before Him as a sea of hosannas, even as He was rasping for breath, His body hung from three nails?

The pagans of old were wiser than many artists and thinkers of today, for they recognized that poetry had links to heaven. "Not by art does the poet sing," Plato wrote, "but by power divine." Jesus spoke in PARABLES

Stepping Stones

Seeing Similarities

» Write sentences using original metaphors and similes (at least four of each) made from the following phrases.

Example: a dirt road. The dirt road was rutted like a farmer's weathered face.

(*Caution:* To be a metaphor or simile, the items must be dissimilar except in the one respect you are indicating. Don't write, "The frog was bumpy as a toad" or "The police siren screamed like a fire engine." Here are three badly flawed and funny metaphors from the Internet: "John and Mary had never met. They were like two hummingbirds who had also never met." "Her eyes were like two brown circles with big black dots in the center." "The red brick wall was the color of a brick-red Crayola crayon.")

Phrases

- a long braid of hair
- an old woman's hand
- the smell of a coming rainstorm
- a Corvette
- a cat's tongue
- the sound of a chainsaw
- fish eyes
- fire
- morning mist
- umbrellas in a crowd opening all at once

because He knew our true sense of this world depends on our glimpsing the next, shown us by way of a man travelling to a far country or a woman measuring meal. Imaginative language—poetry—trains the mind in faith. For what is faith but divine realities we can only imagine, "the substance of things hoped for, the evidence of things not seen" (Heb. 11:1).

Metaphors and similes are examples of FIGURATIVE LANGUAGE. Years ago, the late Burl Ives, a well-loved folk singer, made the charts with his song, "It's Just My Funny Way of Laughing" ("Your leaving didn't bother me. . . .

I'm really happy as can be"). Figurative language is a funny way of talking; it makes no literal sense. Look at Emily Dickinson's poem, "I'll Tell You How the Sun Rose," from which I quoted earlier:

I'll tell you how the Sun rose—
A Ribbon at a time—
The Steeples swam in Amethyst—
The news, like Squirrels, ran—
The Hills untied their Bonnets—
The Bobolinks—begun—
Then I said softly to myself—
"That must have been the Sun"!
But how he set—I know not—
There seemed a purple stile
That little Yellow boys and girls
Were climbing all the while—
Till when they reached the other side,
A Dominie in Gray—
Put gently up the evening Bars—
And led the flock away—

(Be sure to look up *dominie* in your dictionary. Always keep your dictionary close by—and use it—when you read and write poetry.)

Tell me, if you can, what in the world Miss Dickinson means when she pictures hills untying their bonnets or a purple stile being climbed by yellow boys and girls? To answer, you must think freely about the movement and color of the sun as it shifts throughout the day.

Here are other FIGURES OF SPEECH that frequently appear in literature: PERSONIFICATION, APOSTROPHE, HYPERBOLE, UNDERSTATEMENT, METONYMY, PARADOX, IRONY, SYMBOLISM, and ALLEGORY. We will consider the last three of these in the next chapter.

By personification, we mean depicting non-human things or ideas as if they were human (remember the *person* in personification): “Not even the rain has such small hands” (E. E. Cummings); “waves scribbled and erased a shore” (Robert Siegel). In the *Beowulf* passage mentioned earlier, the battle sword is personified in a later line: “The blade went through all the doomed body. She fell to the floor, *the sword was sweating.*”

In an apostrophe, the poem’s narrator addresses an inanimate object or abstraction as if it were present and alive: “Sadness, you are a silver locket/at my throat” (Linda Parsons). Here’s a famous apostrophe in a poem by the early Romantic poet William Blake:

The Sick Rose

O Rose, thou art sick!
The invisible worm
That flies in the night,
In the howling storm,

Has found out thy bed
Of crimson joy
And his dark, secret love
Does thy life destroy.

A writer using hyperbole, also called OVERSTATEMENT, exaggerates as a way of telling the truth. The lover in Robert Burns’ poem, “Oh, My Love is Like a Red, Red Rose,” is eager to prove the depths of his love to his sweetheart:

So fair art thou, my bonny lass,
So deep in love am I;
And I will love thee still, my dear,
Till a’ the seas gang dry.

Till a’ the seas gang dry, my dear,
And the rocks melt wi’ the sun;
And I will love thee still, my dear,
While the sands o’ life shall run.

We know, of course, that to love someone until the seas run dry or rocks melt with the sun is logically impossible. Yet the poem, through exaggeration, is faithful in conveying a man's affection which seems to him unbounded by space or time. Here's another example, from Psalm 6:6: "All night I made my bed to swim; with my tears I dissolved my couch."

Because poetry is a language of intense feeling, figures of speech are marvelously fitted tools to express the inexpressible. Understatement is another way at getting at such truth. The writer says less to say more: "The grave's a fine and quiet place / But none I think do there embrace." The second of these lines, from the poem "To His Coy Mistress" by the seventeenth-century writer Andrew Marvell, offers a good example of this literary device. Obviously, the dead can do nothing but be dead. By saying, "I think," the speaker of this poem understates the finality of death and with it, love, as a tactic to win a lady's affections.

"My Papa's Waltz," by Theodore Roethke, is another poem (this one, twentieth century) that uses understatement effectively to show a little boy's mixed feelings toward his drunken father—

My Papa's Waltz

The whiskey on your breath
Could make a small boy dizzy;
But I hung on like death;
Such waltzing was not easy.

We romped until the pans
Slid from the kitchen shelf;
My mother's countenance
Could not unfrown itself.

The hand that held my wrist
Was battered on one knuckle;
At every step you missed
My right ear scraped a buckle.

You beat time on my head
With a palm caked hard by dirt,
Then waltzed me off to bed
Still clinging to your shirt.

"Such waltzing was not easy" and "My mother's countenance/Could not unfrown itself" are good examples of getting at truth by saying less. The waltzing was frenzied and chaotic. The mother was distressed. But restrained speech fits the tone of the boy desperate to be loyal, to not be a "sissy" in his father's eyes. (The word *clinging,* by the way, is a powerful illustration of literary compression and deliberate ambiguity. The boy clings both for fear and love, a mixed response to his hard-drinking, tough-fighting papa whose crazy dancing brings both pleasure and pain.)

Back in the sixties, a fellow driving around town in a shiny red Impala might ask his friends how they liked his new set of wheels. He would be using a figure of speech known as METONYMY. It means that a part or something closely associated is used to stand for the thing actually meant: wheels = car. When we recite the Lord's Prayer saying, "Give us this day our daily bread," we understand that the word *bread* signifies any sort of nourishment. "The hand that rocks the cradle rules the world" is an example of a well-known metonymy. Can you explain what *hand* and *cradle* represent?

Stepping Stones

» Think of a man-made object—a hub cap, coffee maker, electric fan, etc., and write about it in your journal so as to give it human qualities. Write it as a story or poem.

Example:
The vacuum cleaner coils in a corner, hungry for dust. The owner, who has always been regular in weekly feedings,

has suddenly become negligent. Dust grows right under the vacuum's nose, delectably dry, but no one comes to turn on the stomach. Day and night, the vacuum hears squalls of awful sound coming from the owner's room, then soft soothing sounds, but never footsteps coming close. Sometimes the metal machine glimpses arms and a bundle passing by into the kitchen. It seems the microwave is getting all the attention, and all the bottles it likes, fed into that big square mouth.

A Poem to Consider

» Read the poem below by Dylan Thomas and write a paragraph discussing his use of metonymy.

The Hand That Signed the Paper Felled a City

The hand that signed the paper felled a city;
Five sovereign fingers taxed the breath,
Doubled the globe of dead and halved a country;
These five kings did a king to death.

The mighty hand leads to a sloping shoulder,
The finger joints are cramped with chalk;
A goose's quill has put an end to murder
That put an end to talk.

The hand that signed the treaty bred a fever,
And famine grew, and locusts came;
Great is the hand that holds dominion over
Man by a scribbled name.

The five kings count the dead but do not soften
The crusted wound nor stroke the brow;
A hand rules pity as a hand rules heaven;
Hands have no tears to flow.

Figure the Figures

» Identify the figures of speech in the following excerpts from poems.

1. "A looter of a wind
   Is yanking the golden apples into the grass."
   (from "Tree of Life" by Marie Luise Kaschnitz)

2. "O death, where is thy sting? O grave, where is thy victory?"
   (1 Cor. 15:55)

3. "He clasps the crag with crooked hands."
   (from "The Eagle" by Alfred, Lord Tennyson)

4. "Brush this sand map from my shoulder."
   (from "Good News" by Greg Kuzma)

5. "I should have been a pair of ragged claws
   Scuttling across the floors of silent seas"
   (from "The Love Song of J. Alfred Prufrock" by T. S. Eliot)

6. "With a swoosh the fire started,
   and little tongues of flame
   shot up like hair bristling
   on the back of a fox"
   (Hannah Lepsch)

4. White Whales and Swimming Hats

To be a Christian is to live by paradox, or apparent contradictions. Death is life, suffering is joy, word is flesh. In your journal, write down as many paradoxes as you can think of from the Bible.

Laurence Perrine, explaining paradox in a poetry textbook, retells Aesop's fable about a traveler seeking shelter in the home of a Satyr

> on a bitter winter night. On entering the Satyr's lodging, he blew on his fingers, and was asked by the Satyr why he did it. "To warm them up," he explained. Later, on being served a piping hot bowl of porridge, he blew also on it, and again was asked why he did it. "To cool it off," he explained. The Satyr thereupon thrust him out of doors, for he would have nothing to do with a man who could blow hot and cold with the same breath.

Naturally, the whole matter can be explained, and so it is with all paradoxes. They appear to be contradictory, but with a closer look, they make sense.

George Herbert, a seventeenth-century poet-pastor renowned for his deep piety and extraordinary art, found paradox fitting ground for his poetry. In "Easter Wings," a poem shaped into two sections, each like wings (see page 97), Herbert uses imagery taken from falconry to suggest themes of man's loss through the fall, and his gain through Christ's resurrection: "[I]f I imp my wing on Thine/Affliction shall advance the flight in me." (To "imp" was to repair the injured wing of a hawk by grafting to it feathers from another bird.) Consider the paradox that affliction brings advancement. This can be understood only by reflecting on the spiritual wealth and improvement we have in Jesus Christ when we are grafted onto Him.

The last two figures of speech we will examine—IRONY and SYMBOLISM—are subtle literary devices that open up layers of meaning. Irony can be pictured as a two-way glass in which one person is looking through a window that the other sees as a mirror. Irony involves some kind of discrepancy between what appears to be and what actually is.

VERBAL IRONY occurs when words mean something other than what they say, and quite often, the actual opposite. Mark Antony, in Shakespeare's *Julius Caesar*, delivers a famous speech in which he repeats over and over, "But Brutus is an honorable man." By the end of the speech, the Roman crowd is overwhelmingly convinced that Brutus is anything but honorable. Anarchy follows.

DRAMATIC IRONY refers to a situation where the reader or audience knows more than the character, arousing in us feelings of pity or dread. Poor Job. See him sitting cross-legged in the dust scratching his sores with pottery shards as if to say, "Huh?" We, of course, know better. We are privy to the councils of heaven wherein God makes a pact with Satan to prove you can't keep a righteous man down. Job will come out all right. What's true for Job, of course, is true for us. When the going gets rough, remember that God is on the other side of the mirror.

IRONY OF SITUATION (also called COSMIC IRONY) means a gap between what we expect and what actually happens.

It is ironic that after you work and save for six months to buy a longed-for German shepherd puppy, your father's company transfers him to another location where you will be living in an apartment that forbids pets. O'Henry's famous story, "Gift of the Magi," poignantly illustrates this type of irony. For love, Della sells her hair to buy a watch chain for her husband, Jim, who sells his watch to buy her a comb.

SYMBOLS are images that radiate meanings, like circles set in motion by a stone tossed into a lake. Fire, snake, blood, garden, ocean, sun—all these have been used by poets throughout the ages to touch our basic fears and longings. The ice at the bottom of hell (the *Inferno*), the great white whale (*Moby Dick)*, and the scarlet A in Hawthorne's novel are powerful symbols of the vast, mysterious darkness within and without us, the force we call evil. Good has its typology, too, as in the garden of *Paradise Lost* which, before Adam's fall, represents extravagant, sensuous beauty and holy ground where God walks with man. Notice again that symbols are *images,* that they have *literal meaning* (Melville created Moby Dick as a real whale), and that they point like rays of the sun to larger meanings. In fact, a symbol is a whole quiver of metaphorical arrows pointing upward.

Think of the worm in Blake's poem "The Sick Rose," which we saw in the previous chapter. On the literal level, the worm is a garden pest that destroys a beautiful flower. But there are clues to let us know Blake has more in mind. For one thing, it is an "invisible worm." This gets us to thinking about the unseen world, the spiritual world. It "flies in the night" as if on a covert mission. Night suggests darkness and evil. So does "the howling storm." This is scary, but it gets scarier. The worm "finds out" the rose's secret bed. "Found out" suggests intentionality. This worm is one bad fellow! He's a predator, a seducer. The rose, of course, is a conventional symbol for beauty and love.

ALLEGORY differs from symbolism in that the content of the literary work corresponds to some other meaning beneath the surface. It is, in short, another way of telling an old story. A parable is a kind of allegory, being a small story with a secondary meaning. *Pilgrim's Progress* is probably the most famous allegory, for Christian's journey is a spiritual pilgrimage as well as a literal one. Every aspect of the narrative corresponds with a biblical truth. George Herbert's poem "Redemption" is allegorical, for notions of the Old and New Covenants underlie the tenant's story. After you read it, go back and find theological parallels—

Redemption

Having been tenant long to a rich Lord,
Not thriving, I resolvèd to be bold,
And make a suit unto him, to afford
A new small-rented lease and cancel the old.
In heaven at his manor I him sought:
They told me there that he was lately gone
About some land which he had dearly bought
Long since on earth, to take possession.
I straight returned, and knowing his great birth,
Sought him accordingly in great resorts;
In cities, theaters, gardens, parks, and courts:
At length I heard a ragged noise and mirth
Of thieves and murderers; there I him espied,
Who straight, "Your suit is granted," said, and died.

To sum up our discussion of figurative language, keep in mind that poetry is a language of compression and that figures of speech are one of the primary ways in which poets pack meaning into a small space.

A line from the ancient Scottish ballad, "Sir Patrick Spense," illustrates this idea. Like King David in the Old Testament who sent Uriah off to the battle front, knowing his death was certain, so the king in the ballad deliberately sent Sir Patrick Spence out to sea on a fatal mission during the stormiest time of year:

O our Scots nobles wer richt laith (loath)
  To weet their cork-heild schoone, (wet, shoes)
But lang owre a' the play wer playd,
  Their hats they swam aboone. (above)

To say, "Their hats they swam aboone," is poetry at its best: an image of hats floating on the sea tells the entire tragedy of Sir Patrick and his brave lords.

Figures of speech—metaphor, simile, personification, apostrophe, metonymy, paradox, irony, allegory, and symbolism—enable us to see with new eyes what has always been before us. Percy Bysshe Shelley said, "Poetry lifts the veil from the hidden beauty of the world and makes familiar objects be as if they were not familiar." It is this element of surprise that Jesus used to such great effect in his parables to make fallen human beings perceive their nakedness and need. Figures of speech come from the garden, not the toad part of our brain. Knowing how they work and using them in your writing will deepen your vision of this world and the next.

Stepping Stones

Poems Under Glass

Here are a number of poems, some of which have been partially quoted in our treatment of figurative language. All of them rely on various figures of speech.

» Begin with the poem below, written by the Romantic writer mentioned earlier, Shelley. As always, when you read a poem, consider the situation (if there is one), the speaker, and the poet's purpose. Now examine the poem for its use of dramatic irony.

Ozymandias

I met a traveler from an antique land
Who said: Two vast and trunkless legs of stone
Stand in the desert. Near them, the sand,
Half sunk, a shattered visage lies, whose frown,
And wrinkled lip, and sneer of cold command,
Tell that its sculptor well those passions read
Which yet survive, stamped on these lifeless things,
The hand that mocked them and the heart that fed;
And on the pedestal these words appear:
"My name is Ozymandias, king of kings:
Look on my works, ye Mighty and despair!"
Nothing beside remains. Round the decay
Of that colossal wreck, boundless and bare
The lone and level sands stretch far away.

» Discuss the symbol of the starling in Richard Wilbur's poem "The Writer." It would be helpful first to paraphrase the poem, to identify the speaker, subject, and situation. Be sure to consider the symbol in light of the meaning of the poem as a whole.

The Writer

In her room at the prow of the house
Where light breaks, and the windows are tossed
  with linden,
My daughter is writing a story.

I pause in the stairwell, hearing
From her shut door a commotion of typewriter keys
Like a chain hauled over a gunwale.

Young as she is, the stuff
Of her life is a great cargo, and some of it heavy:
I wish her a lucky passage.

But now it is she who pauses,
As if to reject my thought and its easy figure.
A stillness greatens, in which
The whole house seems to be thinking,
And then she is at it again with a bunched clamor
Of strokes, and again is silent.

I remember the dazed starling
Which was trapped in that very room, two years ago;
How we stole in, lifted a sash

And retreated, not to affright it;
And how for a helpless hour, through the crack of
  the door,
We watched the sleek, wild, dark

An iridescent creature
Batter against the brilliance, drop like a glove
To the hard floor, or the desk-top.

And wait then, humped and bloody,
For the wits to try it again; and how our spirits
Rose when, suddenly sure,

It lifted off from a chair-back,
Beating a smooth course for the right window
And clearing the sill of the world.

It is always a matter, my darling,
Of life or death, as I had forgotten. I wish
What I wished you before, but harder.

» Explain how irony of situation is used in "Is My Team Ploughing" by A. E. Housman. Can you identify the two metonymies in stanza three?

Is My Team Ploughing

"Is my team ploughing,
 That I was used to drive
And hear the harness jingle
 When I was man alive?"

Aye, the horses trample,
 The harness jingles now;
No change though you lie under
 The land you used to plough.

"Is football playing
 Along the river shore,

With lads to chase the leather,
 Now I stand up no more?"

Aye, the ball is flying,
 The lads play heart and soul;
The goal stands up, the keeper
 Stands up to keep the goal.

"Is my girl happy,
 That I thought hard to leave,
And has she tired of weeping
 As she lies down at eve?"

Aye, she lies down lightly,
 She lies not down to weep:
Your girl is well contented.
 Bestill, my lad, and sleep.

"Is my friend hearty,
 Now I am thin and pine;
And has he found to sleep in
 A better bed than mine?"

Aye, lad, I lie easy,
 I lie as lads would choose;
I cheer a dead man's sweetheart.
 Never ask me whose.

» Compare the two poems below, both about important women. Which is more imaginative and genuine?

Mother's Love

Did you ever come to the place
When life seemed naught to you,
When your heart is filled with sorrow,
And friends are mighty few;
When your faith in man is shaken,
And everything seems a fraud,
Till at last you grow indifferent
And doubt the love of God?
At one time you were happy,
Had faith in all mankind;

But one by one your friends proved false—
Faith now is left behind;
'Tis now you start to wandering
Like a dog without a home,
And a kick here and a kick there
As on and on you roam.

The friends whom once you thought were true
Now seem to know you not.
The kindly things you did for them,
Each one has been forgot.
While you were prosperous—you were fit
To live and walk with them,
But when misfortune frowned on you,
They were ready to condemn.
But there is one who still remains
As true as the stars above;
No matter how debased you are,
You still have mother's love.
Though you may sink deep into sin,
Beside God, there is one other
Who is so willing to forgive—
That one is your dear mother.

—Ross B. Clapp

Keeper of the Vines

"I am the Vine, you are the branches . . ." John 15:5

If she had known
as she clutched the two roots close
in her rough hands
on the ship that shivered over swells
and groaned into watery caverns
and bore her up,
scarcely breathing—

If she had known
as she stood, planted
like a small mast on the deck,
homespun sails billowing with hope
through the gray mists,

her prayers mingling with
the mocking cry of grackles rising
above Ireland's rocky coast—

If she had known when,
transplanted and heeled-in,
she plowed her new fields
and grappled her wide dreams
down to earth,
stumbling over stones
and torn by thorns—
If she had known then
all she came to know
and what she could not know
of briary branches she would grow,
would she still have come?

—Rebecca B. Morecraft

5. Musical Thought

As we have seen so far, poetry has certain fundamental characteristics. It uses language imaginatively and with compression. Individual words are valued like rare collectibles and are often chosen for sensory appeal. The arrangement of words—both in proximity to each other and in the way they constitute the poetic line—are critical aspects of the art, as well. Sir Philip Sidney, writing in the sixteenth century, said the poet "cometh to you with words set in delightful proportion." Furthermore, poetry draws from the springs of human emotion. Here we think of the Romantic writer William Wordsworth, who defined poetry as "the spontaneous overflow of powerful feelings recollected in tranquility."

But there is another dimension that has been recognized from ancient times, and that is the moral aspect. "To delight and instruct," that is the aim of poetry, wrote John Dryden in the seventeenth century. Many contemporary poets agree that poetry, by nature, is a teacher and has wisdom to impart (or not, depending on the beliefs of the poet).

Picture the poet as the CEO of WordWorks, Inc. Everyone has a job to do. The Body Builder has his work cut out for him: go for the power words, strong nouns and verbs.

Bring along a Senses Taker for the visual, auditory, tactile, and olfactory concerns. Be back for the noon meeting with Heart. If Heart's not happy, ain't nobody happy. She'll

Stepping Stones

Noisy Words

» Go to a noisy, busy place. Close your eyes and imagine you are blind. For twenty minutes, listen to the sounds around you. Now describe them in your journal. Find words that recreate the sounds. Do the same for a quiet place.

Example: Let's say you chose a laundromat for your busy place. Here is what you might have written:

> *Sitting in an orange plastic chair in the Soak 'n Suds Washorama. Eyes closed. Jukebox blasting an oldy, "Achy Breaky Heart." Voices sounding chewed up like a cow's cud. Rolling and thumping of clothes in dryers. Whooshing, swishing, spraying sound of washers. Jangle of coins. Little kid screeching for bubble gum. Mom scolding. All of this is enough to break your ears—if not your heart!*

rummage through everyone's briefcase and dump those words lacking appropriate emotional weight. On the way out the door, be sure to look in the Mirror of Wisdom. Behind the artful figures of speech, the dazzling displays of language and imagination, is there a moral center? Does the poem illumine?

There's another important member of the team we haven't formally met, and that's the Sound Man. This word-associate specializes in a diverse range of effects: EUPHONY, CACOPHONY, ONOMATOPOEIA, ASSONANCE, CONSONANCE, ALLITERATION, and RHYME. He's fond of saying, "Poetry without music is sawdust and sand. It's cornflakes minus milk." On his wall hangs a plaque with a quote from the Victorian writer Thomas Carlyle: "Poetry, therefore, we will call musical thought."

To be a poet is to have a well-tuned ear, one that hears the music of words and selects those that suit the poem's meaning.

If some of your sounds were harsh and clashing, they are said to be CACOPHONOUS. "Screeching" and "scolding" are good examples. "Cacophonous" is from the Greek prefix *kak,* which means "bad," and *phone*, which means "sound."

Identify cacophony in Fred Chappell's poem "My Grandmother Washes Her Vessels," which takes place in a dairy:

> In the white-washed medical-smelling milkhouse
> She wrestled clanging steel; grumbled and trembled,
> Hoisting the twenty-gallon cans to the ledge
> Of the spring-run (six by three, a concrete grave
> Of slow water). Before she toppled them in—
> Dented armored soldiers booming in pain—
> She stopped to rest . . .

Notice the harsh consonants, particularly the g's: "wrestled clanging steel; grumbled and trembled." Then comes the amazing metaphor of "Dented armored soldiers booming in pain," along with the splendid sound-word, "booming."

Other sounds may have been harmonious and pleasing; these are said to be EUPHONIOUS. (*Eu-* comes from several linguistic roots that combine to mean "well" and "easily.")

Now let's look at a poem by William Butler Yeats. The speaker is planning a dream cabin on a paradisical island. The sounds are altogether euphonious:

The Lake Isle of Innisfree

I will arise and go now, and go to Innisfree,
And a small cabin build there, of clay and wattles made;
Nine bean rows will I have there, a hive for the honey bee,
And live alone in the bee-loud glade.

And I shall have some peace there, for peace comes
  dropping slow,
Dropping from the veils of the morning to where the
  cricket sings;
There midnight's all a glimmer, and noon a purple glow,
And evening full of the linnet's wings.

I will arise and go now, for always night and day
I hear lake water lapping with low sounds by the shore;
While I stand on the roadway, or on the pavements gray,
I hear it in the deep heart's core.

Notice in particular the drawn-out vowel sounds and pleasing accents of the second stanza, and the recreation of watery sounds in the last.

Whether it is a conscious or unconscious act, poets use various means to achieve sound effects. One is ONOMATOPOEIA, defined as words which sound like that which they represent: "hiss" for steam, "buzz" for chainsaw, "gurgle" for water, "crackle" for fire. Edgar Allan Poe's poem "The Bells" captures the growing clamor and dread of bells that begin in silver merriment and end in iron horror. Here's a sample:

Hear the sledges with the bells—
    Silver bells!
What a world of merriment their melody foretells!
How they tinkle, tinkle, tinkle,
    In the icy air of night!
    While the stars that oversprinkle
    All the heavens, seem to twinkle
With a crystalline delight;
    Keeping time, time time,

In a sort of Runic rhyme,
To the tintinnabulation that so musically wells
From the bells, bells, bells, bells,
Bells, bells, bells—
From the jingling and the tinkling of the bells.

ASSONANCE is a device wherein vowel sounds within close proximity are repeated. "Feed/sheet," "stick/lift," "boot/moon" are examples. CONSONANCE refers to repetition of end consonants, as in "shock/cheek," "fallen/melon," "voyage/sewage," "wave/love" (sound, not spelling, is the defining factor). ALLITERATION is the word for repetition of initial and/or internal consonants, as in "rascals wrestling in the road" and "follow the sailor to Manila." Here are lines from the medieval ROMANCE *Sir Gawain and the Green Knight*. Find alliterated words:

And in guise all of green, the gear and the man:
A coat cut close, that clung to his sides,
And a mantle to match, made with a lining
Of furs cut and fitted—the fabric was noble,
Embellished all with ermine, and his hood beside,
That was loosed from his locks, and laid on his shoulders.

Alliteration was heavily used in ancient times as an aid to recitation. Long narrative poems like *Beowulf* and *Sir Gawain* were orally delivered by bards to non-literate audiences. Alliteration also served to unify and enliven the poetic lines, which were unrhymed. Poets today tend to use it in more subtle ways: "narrow strip of darkness" (Stuart Dybek), and "Last night's killing frost uncolored the whole of the Skagit" (Luci Shaw). If you look back at "The Lake Isle of Innisfree," you can find examples of all three of these devices: alliteration, assonance, and consonance.

Of all the sound effects used in poetry, the kind you are probably most familiar with is RHYME (also spelled "rime"):

The days are short,
The sun a spark
Hung thin between
The dark and dark.

—John Updike

"Spark" and "dark" are EXACT RHYMES because the sound is exactly the same except for the initial consonants. They are also called END RHYMES (coming at the ends of lines) as opposed to INTERNAL RHYME, where the rhyming words are found within the line: "All is seared with trade; bleared, smeared with toil."

Use of end rhyme in poetry has declined in the twentieth century. For one thing, the same rhymes were used so often they lost their freshness and achieved the level of cliché as in "God/sod," "dream/stream," "heaven/seven," etc. For another, many poets feel that rhyme forces them to use certain words that may not be the most suitable for the poem's purpose. Suppose I want to use *orange* at the end of a line. If writing a rhymed poem, I can't. There is no word that rhymes with orange.

To get around these obstacles, writers often use SLANT RHYME—also called APPROXIMATE RHYME. *Orange* might be rhymed with *strange,* and *easy* with *dizzy* (the latter rhyme appears in "My Papa's Waltz," seen earlier). With slant rhyme, the vowel sounds are different; the final consonant is the same. (Slant rhyme and consonance are the same thing.) Emily Dickinson, regarded as the mistress of slant, used the device to great effect, as in her poem "A Narrow Fellow in the Grass." See if you can spot the slant rhymes. Identify exact rhymes, too.

A narrow fellow in the grass
Occasionally rides—
You may have met him? Did you not,
His notice instant is:

The grass divides as with a comb,
A spotted shaft is seen,
And then it closes at your feet
And opens further on:

He likes a boggy acre,
A floor too cool for corn,
But when a boy, and barefoot,
I more than once at noon

Have passed, I thought, a whip-lash
Unbraiding in the sun,
When, stooping to secure it,
It wrinkled, and was gone.

Several of nature's people
I know, and they know me;
I feel for them a transport
Of cordiality;

But never met this fellow,
Attended or alone,
Without a tighter breathing
And zero at the bone.

Another way to avoid the artificiality of exact rhymes is to use ENJAMBMENT, or run-over lines. Instead of ending a sentence at the close of the line (this is called an END-STOPPED line), writers sometimes carry the sentence over into the next. This takes attention off the rhyme, pulling you along into the next line. *Below* and *know* are subtle rhymes because of this effect:

Old Eben Flood, climbing alone one night
Over the hill between the town below
And the forsaken upland hermitage
That held as much as he should ever know
On earth again of home, paused warily.

—E. A. Robinson

Incidentally, when you read poetry aloud (a necessity!), don't pause at the end of the line unless there is a comma, period, or some other signal from the writer to indicate a stop.

A final word about rhyme: in writing poetry, your main emphasis should be on imagery and figurative language while training your ear to select words for their sound effects. Rhyme, if it is to be adopted, should come later, and be used in fresh and subtle ways.

An important element of the use of sound in poetry is suitability to purpose. An oft-quoted passage from Alexander Pope expresses the concept well:

> True ease in writing comes from art, not chance,
> As those move easiest who have learned to dance.
> 'Tis not enough no harshness gives offense,
> The sound must seem an echo to the sense.

What is Pope saying here? A good writer is one who selects words intelligently and from the springs of creative consciousness. The effect is one of effortlessness, like Michael Jordan performing on the basketball court.

Study the following poem by Robert Morgan for sounds as they are wedded to sense:

Apple Count

A late summer sound, of apples
falling in the dark, one breaking
loose and the branch swishing release
as the ripe weight knocks leaves and limbs
below and ricochets to hard
ground, piling with others into
a depression where yellowjackets
gather tunneling bruised skin. And
another drops in random but
precise rhythm, rolling a limb
to the wet grass. It is the sound

of large melting, of red drops formed
on twigs all summer and letting
go the work of bee and sun, leaf
and petal, coming down on their
own in the night and yielding
to the still hungry earth. There one
goes again and the limb shakes back
into place, freed a little, to
rest among crickets, among clouds.

Stepping Stones

As you gain tools of the poetic trade, you want your writing to reflect what you've learned. Here are some projects to help you develop an attentive ear. Choose two or three.

Hear, Hear

» Take a fairy tale or other well-known story and write it as an alliterated poem in ACCENTUAL METER like that used in Sir Gawain and the Green Knight. In accentual meter, every line has the same number of accented syllables. You can have as many unaccented ones as you like.

» Write a poem recreating an activity in which noise plays an important part.

Suggestions: Watching fireworks, swimming in a public pool, singing in a choir, viewing a construction sight, bowling, sitting in a stadium during a game.

» Memorize "The Lake Isle of Innisfree," and recite it with proper expression.

» Using slant rhyme, write a 6–8 line poem about an insect (study a real one first).

» Write a pair of companion poems, one called "Euphony" and the other "Cacophony." Personify euphony and cacophony. Decide which is male and which female. Let each speak its own sounds. Choose images that you associate with these concepts.

» Listen to a selection of classical music, something that evokes strong emotion. In your journal write images and ideas that come to mind, then transform these into a poem.

6. Anatomy Lessons

One of the most extraordinary moments in a woman's life is to hear her unborn baby's heartbeat. There it is, a drum the size of a crumb keeping the tempo of stars—proof enough this is not a dream but a resident inhabiting the body's most private room. The heart's clockwork is one of the great mysteries of creation. Indeed, all of creation is rhythmic, from the movement of tides to the snoring of a man in a hammock. Rain patters rhythmically; cicadas keep time like a thousand shaking castanets. We human beings are born to rhythm. Look how we tap our feet to tunes and rock back and forth sitting still.

Poetry is a rhythmic language that draws on the cadences of speech. What do we mean by RHYTHM? The word refers to the ebb and flow of sound. In language, this means repetition of accented and unaccented syllables (also called stresses and unstresses). When rhythm is arranged systematically, falling at regular intervals, it is called METER. Metrical poetry is called VERSE. The units of accented and unaccented syllables are referred to as FEET. Meters and feet are given specific names, odd names like dimeter, iambs, and trochees. To identify these and determine the pattern is to SCAN the poem. Overall, the study of this strange music is called PROSODY. And what's the use of it? In one sense, not much. As the twentieth-century poet T. S. Eliot said, "a study of anatomy will not teach you how to make a hen lay eggs." He went on to say that it is by studying *poems*, not poetry, that one learns to write.

But there are sound reasons for studying the anatomy of a poem. By doing so, you will be aided in your discovery of its inner dynamics—its spirit, so to speak—and this insight fits you for your apprenticeship as a writer. You will come to see that Milton needed grandeur for *Paradise Lost* and thus rejected what he called "vulgar rhyme" in favor of BLANK VERSE.

You admire the Hebrews for their parallels of thought that sometimes agree and sometimes oppose and work like pistons to create energy. You recognize that most verses published in greeting cards and in *The World's Best-Loved Poems* follow a sing-song rhythm that fails to surprise, fails to disturb, and fails to lift any sort of veil from the world's mystery. Thus you learn you do not write doggerel. Furthermore, by studying the metrical geography of a given work with its system of stresses, you discover what places in the poem matter most. As X. J. Kennedy says, "Stresses embody meanings." In short, just as a ballet dancer masters forms, and the artist, the fundamentals of line, so the aspiring poet learns the talk of his shop and experiments with various patterns to improve his craft.

Consider the admirable uses of rhythm in the following poem by Henry W. Longfellow:

The Tide Rises, The Tide Falls

The tide rises, the tide falls,
The twilight darkens, the curlew calls;
Along the sea-sands damp and brown
The traveller hastens toward the town,
   And the tide rises, the tide falls.

Darkness settles on roofs and walls,
But the sea, the sea in the darkness calls;
The little waves, with their soft, white hands,
Efface the footprints in the sands,
    And the tide rises, the tide falls.

The morning breaks; the steeds in their stalls
Stamp and neigh, as the hostler calls;
The day returns, but nevermore
Returns the traveller to the shore,
    And the tide rises, the tide falls.

Try listening to a lecture or sermon as if you had never heard English before. Listen for the flow of syllables—some strong, some weak. What do we mean by an accented syllable? Is it louder? Does it take longer to pronounce than its neighboring syllable does?

Actually, four phonetic properties belong to every syllable we utter. These are pitch (high or low sound), loudness, length (how long it takes to pronounce the syllable), and timbre (this refers to the quality of sound—fuzziness, breathiness, sharpness, hoarseness).

Scholars tell us that the most prominent sound pattern in English is an unstressed syllable followed by a stressed one. When used as a deliberate pattern in a poem, it is called an iamb, one of several FEET, or syllabic unites available to poets. Of course in speech the pattern is random and inconsistent. In poetry, iambic meter—presenting the pattern at regular intervals—has historically been the prevailing one. Other feet are the trochee (opposite of the iamb: stress, followed by unstress), anapest (two unstresses followed by a stress), the dactyl (a stress followed by two unstresses), and the spondee (two stresses). The stresses (also called accents) are indicated with an accent mark. The unstresses are given this mark, (˘). Here are the feet with examples:

IAMB	Thĕre is´/ă foun´/tăin filled´/wĭth blood´
TROCHEE	Ti´ gĕr/ti´ gĕr/burn´iñg bright´
ANAPEST	Tw̆as thĕ night´/bĕfŏre Christ ´/măs whĕn all´/ thrŏugh thĕ house´
DACTYL	Soft´lў ănd/ten´dĕrlў/Je´sŭs ĭs/call´iñg
SPONDEE	old´ crow´

Stepping Stones

Iamb What Iamb

» Here's something fun and kind of crazy to do: draw the feet. Think of what an iamb looks like, a trochee, and so forth. Use colored pencils. Don't try to be logical about this!

In scanning a poem, we figure out which foot is *dominant*. Good poets generally break step to keep their rhythms from becoming too sing-songish, so don't be thrown by lines that depart from the main meter. One qualifying word: scansion is an inexact process because sound is subjective and emphasis is often a matter of degree. But generally, we can describe the metrical pattern followed by a poet. After determining the foot, we tell how many feet occur per line. Once we have done this, we can name the line as follows:

one foot	MONOMETER	five feet	PENTAMETER
two feet	DIMETER	six feet	HEXAMETER
three feet	TRIMETER	seven feet	HEPTAMETER
four feet	TETRAMETER	eight feet	OCTAMETER

What we end up with is this formula: FOOT + LINE = METER.

Now let's scan the first stanza of "A Birthday," by the Victorian poet Christina Rossetti. Read it aloud, exaggerating the stresses. Can you identify the foot and line?

My heart is like a singing bird
    Whose nest is in a watered shoot:
My heart is like an apple tree
    Whose boughs are bent with thickset fruit;
My heart is like a rainbow shell
    That paddles in a halcyon[1] sea;
My heart is gladder than all these
    Because my love is come to me.

If you said iambic tetrameter, you were right. The first line and those following contain four iambs—an unstressed followed by a stressed syllable.

My̆ heart´/is̆ like´/ă sing´/inğ bird´
    Whŏse nest´/is̆ in´/ă wa´/tĕred shoot´.

Here is another segment of a poem for you to scan—from "Snow in Spring" by Ivy O. Eastwick:

Feather on feather
on feather it falls,
white on the chimney pots,
rooftops and walls,
soft on the mountainside,
bright on the tree—
goose-feather snowflakes
all lovely and free

Stepping Stones

Write to the Beat

» Using one of the meters described, write a poem about one of the following: eating watermelon, wading in the ocean, climbing a tree, falling asleep.

Counting Out Rhyme

» Scan the poem on the next page, marking the stresses and unstresses. Determine the meter. Notice also the use of enjambment.

[1] Be sure to look up *halcyon* in the dictionary.

Counting Out Rhyme

Silver bark of beech, and sallow
Bark of yellow birch and yellow
  Twig of willow.

Stripe of green in moosewood maple,
Color seen in leaf of apple,
  Bark of popple.

Wood of popple pale as moonbeam,
Wood of oak for yoke and barn-beam,
  Wood of hornbeam.

Silver bark of beech, and hollow
Stem of elder, tall and yellow
  Twig of willow.

—Edna St. Vincent Millay

Do you see that the predominant foot in the Eastwick poem is the dactyl? (Fea´thĕr ŏn/fea´thĕr) The first two lines, containing one dactyl each, are dactylic monometer. The third and fifth lines are dactylic dimeter (two dactyls). This pattern alternates throughout the poem. Consider how meter is related to the sense of the poem. The poet has found a rhythm to match the movement of snowflakes.

Long ago, in the shadows of the past, poetry was spoken or sung by a bard or scop beside the hearth or in a mead hall to rapt audiences hungry for adventures and geography, for warriors and giants and strong, beautiful women, for moral grandeur and lofty language—all this to carry them out of their everyday world of struggle and sorrow, to gladden their hearts, transmit their history and remind them of divine purpose. With the technological revolution begun by the printing press and continuing today with electronic media, poetry has been more a matter of the printed page. Even so, poetry will always retain its relation to sound or else atrophy (waste away), as Ezra Pound said.

It is good first to read a poem silently. Then read it aloud to yourself or someone else. Read poems at the dinner table or on the front porch. Read with energy and expression. Read slowly and articulate individual words. If it's a rhymed poem, avoid a sing-song rhythm. Follow the poem where it leads. Stop at the end of a line only if terminal punctuation requires it. Pause at commas. A pause in the middle of the line indicated by punctuation is called a CAESURA. For a good example of one, go back and look at Robert Morgan's "Apple Count" (page 60–61). Line 11 contains a caesura, following the word "ground." Can you identify another caesura in the poem?

The poems in this book are good ones to read aloud. The poems *you* write as you study this book are even better for you to recite. Organize a reading for family and friends featuring you and another poet or two you might invite.

Attend a poetry reading. Well-known writers often give readings at colleges, universities, and libraries. Call the English department at a local college and ask for any scheduled readings. You can also go to the library and check out recordings of poets reading their work. Or, look on the internet where poets both famous and obscure can be heard reading poetry. When I was in graduate school (a creative writing program), we would listen with ecstasy to Dylan Thomas records. Poetry is delicious. Devour it.

7. A Few Formalities: Sonnet, Haiku, and Syllabic Verse

St. Augustine wrote of God as being "the one alone from whom is every manner of form." What is form but a river bank, a beehive, a right angle, a rooster's crow? It is the shape of sound, the curve of space, the Word made flesh. Form is the incarnation of idea, the sum of all parts. Form is the garden where the real toads live.

Wait, you say. What you're talking about here is sonnets, right? Sonnets, yes. And terza rima, blank verse, haiku, pantoum, sestina, ballade, villanelle. Think of these poetic forms as clay pots of different sizes and shapes—some very small, some with narrow necks, some square, some squat. Poets throughout time and the world have developed molds to fit words into. These molds are called CLOSED, FIXED, or RECEIVED forms. The beauty of writing formal poetry is that it admits you into a stream that has been running for a long time. Or, to look from another angle, it's as if you were making a quilt following a pattern handed down in your family from many generations.

Closed form presses the mind into thought- shapes the mind would not have otherwise conceived. One writer, Richard Wilbur, compares it to a genie in a bottle, its power owing to the pressure of confinement. When successfully done, the mold is invisible. The seams do not show. The poem has a kind of inevitability, as if it could not have been written another way. (Actually, all worthwhile art has this quality.)

FREE FORM, also called OPEN FORM and FREE VERSE, is not formless. Rather, the poet makes up his or her own design. There is no fixed meter, no defined line length or syllabic structure. But there is attention to sound and the rhythms of language. Ezra Pound, the father of modern poetry, said that poets should "compose in the sequence of the musical phrase, not in the sequence of the metronome." With free form, the way the poem looks on the page is important, with white space often used creatively. Here is an example from E. E. Cummings:

Chanson Innocente[1]

in Just-
spring when the world is mud-
luscious the little
lame balloonman

whistles far and wee

and eddieandbill come
running from marbles and
piracies and it's
spring

when the world is puddle-wonderful

the queer
old balloonman whistles
far and wee
and bettyandisbel come dancing

from hop-scotch and jump-rope and

[1] Innocent Song

it's
spring
and
    the

        goat-footed

balloonMan whistles
far
and
wee

Why does he crunch certain words together? Why does he use white space as he does? Think about the child-like perspective of the poem and how it is achieved.

We will talk more about free verse in chapter nine, but for now, let's take a closer look at fixed forms. By studying these, you can appreciate the artistry of poets who embrace the challenge of hard literary tasks and find their voices in stricture—what Diane Ackerman calls "dancing in chains." And you, too, can wade in the stream of literary tradition, writing your own sonnets and pantoums.

The fourteen-line SONNET is perhaps the best known English form, originating not in England but in Italy in the thirteenth century. It was the favorite of Francesco Petrarch, a poet and early figure of the Renaissance who wrote passionate verses to the lady Laura. Known as the PETRARCHAN OF ITALIAN SONNET, this poem follows a set rhyme scheme as follows: *abbaabba cdcdcd*. Rhyme design is indicated by alphabetical letters. Each letter represents a different rhyme and is written beside it in the right margin. For example, next to the end rhyme "small," you would write *a*. Let's say the next line ends with a new rhyme, the word "light." Beside it you would write *b*. The third line ends with "wall," which is rhyme *a*, the fourth, with "night," which is *b*, and so forth.

The first eight-line section of the Italian sonnet is called the OCTAVE. The second of six is the SESTET. Some variation is allowed in the sestet. An alternate pattern is *cdecde*. What is the idea of these divisions? Here is an explanation found in Hibbard and Holman's *A Handbook to Literature:*

> The octave bears the burden; a doubt, a problem, a reflection, a query, an historical statement, a cry of indignation or desire, a vision of the idea. The sestet eases the load, resolves the problem or doubt, answers the query, solaces the yearning, realizes the vision.

In England, the sonnet was altered to fit a more varied rhyme scheme since English has fewer rhyming words than Italian. The SHAKESPEAREAN SONNET (also known as the ENGLISH SONNET), named for the great playwright and poet, follows the rhyme scheme *abab cdcd efef gg.* The paired rhyme at the end (called a COUPLET) is typically a commentary on the preceding lines of the poem. Most sonnets, English and Italian, are written in iambic pentameter.

Study the sonnet below. Mark the rhymes with matching alphabetical letters. Tell which type of sonnet it is—

On His Blindness

When I consider how my light is spent
Ere half my days in this dark world and wide,
And that one talent which is death to hide
Lodged with me useless, though my soul more bent
To serve therewith my Maker, and present
My true account, lest he returning chide,
"Doth God exact day-labor, light denied?"
I fondly ask. But Patience, to prevent
That murmur, soon replies, "God doth not need
Either man's work or his own gifts. Who best
Bear his mild yoke, they serve him best. His state

Is kingly: thousands at his bidding speed,
And post o'er land and ocean without rest;
They also serve who only stand and wait."

—John Milton

If you guessed an Italian sonnet, you are correct. Now let's look at an English sonnet by William Shakespeare.

Sonnet 29

When, in disgrace with fortune and men's eyes,
I all alone beweep my outcast state,
And trouble deaf heaven with my bootless cries
And look upon myself and curse my fate,
Wishing me like to one more rich in hope,
Featured like him, like him with friends possess'd,
Desiring this man's art and that man's scope,
With what I most enjoy contented least;
Yet in these thoughts myself almost despising,
Haply I think on thee,—and then my state,
Like to the lark at break of day arising
From sullen earth, sings hymns at heaven's gate;
  For thy sweet love remembered such wealth brings
  That then I scorn to change my state with kings.

Stepping Stones

Edible Sonnets

» Look up more sonnets to read and study. Most great poets past and present have written them. See if you can find a sonnet composed by a twentieth-century poet. Now write a sonnet of your own, either Italian or English. Try using some approximate rhyme. Include two metaphors/similes. Write in the language of our own time. This is very important. Many beginning writers mistakenly adopt what is referred to as POETIC DICTION, an archaic style of writing that "sounds" poetic and includes words and phrases seen in older poetry, usually from the Romantic era: o'er, e'en, 'tis, vale. Novices are also tempted to dress up or "prettify" speech, saying, "The arms of a beauteous tree beckoned scores of winged creatures" instead of "Leaves like gesturing hands drew birds to eat the berries." Remember, it is generally best to avoid abstract words, offering imagery instead.

An idea for your sonnet is to base it on a family feast such as Thanksgiving or Christmas. Include images of food and faces, sounds of voices and song. Don't worry about telling the reader how special this event is. Your own "edible words," to borrow a phrase from Robert Siegel, will say it all. Your closing couplet or sestet should include a final, suggestive image or metaphor such as bread being compared to "good words in our mouths," "and steam rising like blessing from each plate." Note the slant rhyme of "eat" and "plate."

Another received form, this from the Japanese, is HAIKU, a verse form that usually has seventeen syllables. Typically the pattern is 5-7-5, but other variations are followed, too, such as 6-8-4. Writing a haiku is like catching a lightning bug. For an instant, you hold glory, then release it. Haiku, usually taking an image from nature, captures some insight:

The lightning flashes!
And slashing through the darkness,
A night-heron's screech.

—Basho

Fallen flowers rise
back to the branch—I watch:
oh . . . butterflies!

—Moritake

Americans have used haiku in all sorts of ways, adapting the form to their own purposes. Here are two from David Oates:

Tiny raindrops
in my daughter's dark hair—
starry sky.

From mountaintop,
a vision of valleys and hills—
rumpled green blanket.

Below are some haiku written by my students. For this, I asked that the haiku include some sort of motion in nature and a sense of surprise.

A smooth gray pebble
slithers across the rough dirt:
sticky, slimy slug.

—Chris Greene

A speckled spider
running across lines of silk
halted by a twig.

—William Caleb Rutledge

Poisonous spider
weaving a dazzling web,
legs piercing the air.

—Joshua Rutledge

Cat crawling slowly
upon a grey mouse, his prey:
razor teeth ready.

—Candace Johnson

Haiku is a type of SYLLABIC VERSE. This is a form designed by the writer, who chooses in advance how many syllables each line in a STANZA will have and how many lines

Stepping Stones

Do Haiku

» Write a haiku following the 5-7-5 syllabic pattern and follow the instructions I gave my students: choose a scene from nature you have actually observed where there is motion of some kind. Write the haiku, including a sense of surprise.

per stanza. Stanzas, by the way, are a kind of verse paragraph. They are lines of related thought grouped together. We will discuss varieties of stanzas later in the chapter.

One of the most beautiful poems ever written is "Fern Hill" by the twentieth-century poet Dylan Thomas. After reading the poem several times aloud and absorbing its music and lovely dream-like imagery celebrating childhood and lamenting its loss, examine the lines of each stanza. Count the syllables and describe the pattern. You will find that "Fern Hill" follows a strict and complex syllabic pattern—an amazing achievement indeed. I read that Thomas wrote about 400 drafts of this poem before he was satisfied!

Fern Hill

Now as I was young and easy under the apple boughs
About the lilting house and happy as the grass was green,
The night above the dingle starry,
Time let me hail and climb
Golden in the heydeys of his eyes,
And honored among wagons I was prince of
the apple towns
And once below a time I lordly had the trees and leaves
Trail with daisies and barley
Down the rivers of windfall light.

And as I was green and carefree, famous among the
barns

About the happy yard and singing as the farm was home,
In the sun that is young once only,
Time let me play and be
Golden in the mercy of his means,
And green and golden I was huntsman and herdsman,
the calves
Sang to my horn, the foxes on the hills barked clear
and cold,
And the sabbath rang slowly
In the pebbles of the holy streams.

All the sun long it was running, it was lovely, the hay
Fields high as the house, the tunes from the chimneys,
it was air
And playing, lovely and watery
And fire green as grass.
And nightly under the simple stars
As I rode to sleep the owls were bearing the farm away,
All the moon long I heard, blessed among stables,
the nightjars
Flying with the ricks, and the horses
Flashing into the dark.

And then to awake, and the farm, like a wanderer white
With the dew, come back, the cock on his shoulder:
it was all
Shining, it was Adam and maiden,
The sky gathered again
And the sun grew round that very day.
So it must have been after the birth of the simple light
In the first, spinning place, the spellbound horses
walking warm
Out of the whinnying green stable
On to the fields of praise.

And honored among foxes and pheasants by the gay
house
Under the new made clouds and happy as the heart
was long,
In the sun born over and over,
I ran my heedless ways,

My wishes raced through the house high hay
And nothing I cared, at my sky blue trades, that
time allows
In all his tuneful turning so few and such morning songs
Before the children green and golden
Follow him out of grace,

Nothing I cared, in the lamb white days, that time
would take me
Up to the swallow thronged loft by the shadow
of my hand,
In the moon that is always rising,
Nor that riding to sleep
I should hear him fly with the high fields
And wake to the farm forever fled from the
childless land.
Oh as I was young and easy in the mercy of his means,
Time held me green and dying
Though I sang in my chains like the sea.

Stepping Stones

Syllabic Magic

» Devise a syllabic poem of at least four stanzas. Decide how many lines will be in each stanza and how many syllables per line. For your subject, write about a childhood place that was magical to you (under the hydrangea bush, rocking on the porch swing, etc.). It is best to mingle odd and even numbers of syllabic lines.

8. More Formalities

A common way to organize the ideas and images of a poem is through stanzas. In Italian, *stanza* means "a stopping or standing." The idea is that each group of lines, the pattern of which is repeated throughout the poem, is like a room where one stops, as in an art gallery, then moves on to the next room. When reading a poem, consider each stanza individually but also in relation to the lines that precede it. The same applies when you are writing a poem. Build stanzas according to the poem's progression of ideas and images. Once you have established a stanzaic pattern, be consistent. Make sure your stanzas have the same number of lines. You may wish to follow a metrical pattern or rhyme scheme, but it is not required.

The first type of stanza we will examine is the couplet, mentioned in chapter seven. The lines are arranged in pairs and have similar end rhymes. Usually, the lines are the same length. Here's a poem by Nancy Willard written in couplets:

The Cat to His Dinner

Fern and flower, safely keep
this tender mouse I put to sleep.

Let snow and silence mark the site
of my unseemly appetite.

Her bravery, her tiny fall
shall be a model for us all.

May God, Who knows our best and worst,
send me another as good as the first.

The HEROIC COUPLET (also called CLOSED COUPLET) is written in rhyming iambic pentameter. Couplets do not always appear as separate stanzas but may simply be paired lines that form a complete thought as in the final two lines of a Shakespearian sonnet. OPEN COUPLETS are those in which the thought is not complete but is carried over into the next couplet.

Alexander Pope, literary giant of the Neo-Classic age (also called the Age of Reason), favored heroic couplets in his poetry, as in the selection below taken from *An Essay on Criticism,* that instructs in how poetry is to be read and written. Pope is saying that a poet may write technically flawless verse, but without passion and wit, he is no true artist—

A perfect judge will read each work of wit
With the same spirit that its author writ:
Survey the whole, nor seek slight faults to find
Where Nature moves, and rapture warms the mind;
Nor lose, for that malignant dull delight,
The generous pleasure to be charmed with wit.
But in such lays as neither ebb nor flow,
Correctly cold, and regularly low,
That, shunning faults, one quiet tenor keep,
We cannot blame indeed—but we may sleep.

The QUATRAIN, a stanza of four lines, has been described as "the workhorse of English poetry" because of its popular and long-standing use. The lines may be

Stepping Stones

» Write a praise poem in rhyming couplets. Choose related items as your subject: a season of the year, foods, books, clothes, insects, birds, etc. Have sections of couplets, beginning each with "Praise be to God for . . ." and developing the item in each section. Here's an unfinished poem I wrote, to give you an idea of how you might do this:

Praise for Pets

Praise be to God for the furred snake
Called a feline by mistake.

Its green eyes freeze on birds that feed:
Schemer, striker, queen of speed.

Its sneaky tail's a snake, also,
Sinewy, hypnotical.

* * *

Praise be to God for the parakeet
With polka dot beard and skier's feet.

Whose kitchen songs include the chat
Of frying fish and bubbling pot.

unrhymed or rhymed. If rhymed, a number of variations are possible, though the most common is *abab*. Read the following quatrains and describe the rhyme scheme of each, using alphabetical letters as explained earlier.

(from Robert Frost's
"Stopping by Woods on a Snowy Evening")

Whose woods these are I think I know
His house is in the village though;
He will not see me stopping here
To watch his woods fill up with snow.

(from Thomas Hardy's "In Time of 'The Breaking of Nations'")

Only a man harrowing clods
 In a slow silent walk,
With an old horse that stumbles and nods
 Half asleep as they stalk.

(from Frost's "The Pasture")

I'm going out to clean the pasture spring;
I'll only stop to rake the leaves away
(And wait to watch the water clear, I may):
I shan't be gone long.—You come too.

(from Robert Burns's "Ye Flowery Banks")

Ye flowery banks o' bonnie Doon
 How can ye blume sae fair?
How can ye chant, ye little birds,
 And I sae fu' o' care?

A three-line stanza is called a TERCET, OR TRIPLET. The lines all end with the same rhyme. TERZA RIMA is a kind of tercet from Italy that follows an interlocking rhyme scheme: *aba, bcb, cdc, ded,* and so on. It is the pattern Dante uses in *The Divine Comedy.* James Merrill, an American poet, uses terza rima in his long poem, "Transfigured Bird." A sample follows:

That day the eggshell of appearance split
And weak of its own translucence lay in the dew.
A child fond of natural things discovered it.

Though it was broken it was very blue,
Pearly within, and lit by sun enough
For it to glow, though broken clean in two.

He ran home with it wrapped in a handkerchief
To where he kept his findings. Here, in a nest,
Robins' eggs hollowed with a pin and a puff;

Moths spread like ferns, then ferns and flowers pressed
Like moths on cotton; a bullfrog, once green;
Minerals, and a few smutched feathers—lest

The world be part forgotten if part unseen . . .

Mark the rhyme scheme.

RIME ROYAL is a seven-line stanza with iambic pentameter as its meter. Chaucer, Shakespeare, and many other notable poets have used this form.

The SPENSERIAN STANZA was developed by the sixteenth-century poet Edmund Spenser for *The Faerie Queen*. Its characteristic features are: (1) nine lines per stanza, (2) the first eight are iambic pentameter, (3) the ninth is iambic hexameter (six feet), (4) the rhyme scheme is *ababbcbcc:*

At length they chaunst to meet upon the way
An aged Sire, in long blacke weedes yclad,[1]
His feete all bare, his beard all hoarie gray
And by his belt his booke he hanging had;
Sober he seemde, and very sagely sad,
And to the ground his eyes were lowly bent,
Simple in shew, and voyde of malice bad,
And all the way he prayed, as he went,
And often knockt his brest, as one that did repent.

A number of the Romantic poets used the Spenserian stanza to great effect. Consider this stanza taken from John Keats's "The Eve of St. Agnes," a beautiful, sensuous narrative poem based on a legend. According to superstition, on the eve of St. Agnes (she was a martyr and the patron saint of virgins), a dream lover would visit a virtuous maiden and bring her a splendid feast. Besides noting the conventions of the stanza, pay attention to the sumptuous images and sound effects—

[1] yclad: *clad in long black garments*

And still she slept an azure-lidded sleep,
In blanched linen, smooth, and lavendered,
While he from forth the closet brought a heap
Of candied apple, quince, and plum, and gourd;
With jellies soother than the creamy curd,
And lucent syrups, tinct with cinnamon;
Manna and dates, in argosy[2] transferred
From Fez; and spiced dainties, every one,
From silken Samarcand to cedared Lebanon.

An important device poets employ is repetition. Words, phrases, lines, and entire stanzas are repeated for emphasis, symbolic value, or to add music. How does Shakespeare use repetition in these lines from the play *Love's Labor Lost*?

When Icicles Hang by the Wall

When icicles hang by the wall,
And Dick the shepherd blows his nail,
And Tom bears logs into the hall,
And milk comes frozen home in pail,
When blood is nipped and ways be foul,
Then nightly sings the staring owl,
"Tu-whit, tu-who!"
A merry note,
While greasy Joan doth keel[3] the pot.

When all aloud the wind doth blow,
And coughing drowns the parson's saw,
And birds sit brooding in the snow,
And Marian's nose looks red and raw,
When roasted crabs hiss in the bowl,
Then nightly sings the staring owl,
"Tu-whit, tu-who!"
A merry note,
While greasy Joan doth keel the pot.

[2] argosy: *by ship*
[3] keel: *skim*

In Luci Shaw's poem below (a line from which was previously quoted), the repetition of what word adds to meaning? Explain—

Golden Delicious

Last night's killing frost uncolored
the whole of the Skagit. This afternoon,
hiking the valley, I found
a spread of apple trees gone wild—
black nets of branches
heavy with yellow fruit, frozen
solid enough to last the winter.

If the freeze had held them
in its hand, vise-hard, not let go . . .

But a rogue river of wind, come loose
from the Sound at noon, began
to thaw the valley rotten.
Now the numbed apples are falling,
one, one, one, till the gray ground boils
with bruised gold, hanging the old orchard's
autumn air with the winy smell of loss.

The lines of Walt Whitman's poetry are broad, sweeping and cumulative in force. This is achieved through his heaping of details and the use of PARALLELISM, as in the following lines from *Song of Myself*:

Where sun-down shadows lengthen over the limitless
  and lonesome prairie,
Where herds of buffalo make a crawling spread of the
  square miles far and near,
Where the humming-bird shimmers, where the neck of
  the long-lived swan is curving and winding,
Where the laughing-gull scoots by the shore, where she
  laughs her near-human laugh,
Where bee-hives range on a gray bench in the garden half
  hid by the high weeds,

Where band-neck'd partridges roost in a ring on the ground with their heads out,
Where burial coaches enter the arch'd gates of a cemetery,
Where winter wolves bark amid wastes of snow and icicled trees,
Where the yellow-crown'd heron comes to the edge of the marsh at night and feeds upon small crabs,
Where the splash of swimmers and divers cools the warm noon,
Where the katy-did works her chromatic reed on the walnut-tree over the well . . .

There are many other received forms, a number of them French in origin such as the ballade, the villanelle, the sestina, the rondeau and its variants the rondel, roundel, and roundelay. From the Middle East comes the ghazal; from Malaya, the pantoum. Let's look at three of these, the VILLANELLE, SESTINA, and PANTOUM, all examples of interlocking rhymes.

The villanelle is composed of five three-line stanzas and a final four-line stanza. Only two rhyme sounds are

Stepping Stones

Poems from the Rainbow

» In your journal make a list of all the things you can think of that are of a certain color. Here's my blue list:

- the sky
- blue jay
- Wedgewood
- the sea
- physician's scrub suit
- sheets
- a lake
- blue heron
- blueberries
- bruises
- child in pool too long
- smoke
- chickory
- cotton candy
- sadness
- swimming pool
- forget-me-not
- police lights
- Blue Willow
- Windex
- robin's egg
- lapis lazuli
- teacup

Now write a poem using some or all the items in your list. Use a recurring word, phrase, line, or grammatical structure. Arrange the poem in stanzas.

Canvas

With blue the world is draped, blue sheet of sky,
physician's scrub suit rumpled in a corner,
blue fence of chickory by the road,
Ann's Blue Willow platter in a box,
sorrow growing heavy as lake water.

With blue the world is draped, blue wall of sea,
police lights spilling nightmare, blue
of bruises, smoke, blue heron with one leg,
a robin's egg, broken teacup on the walk,
swimming pool, a child's blue mouth.

allowed in the poem. Thus the lines follow this pattern: *aba aba aba aba aba abaa*. The first line is repeated to form lines 6, 12, and 18. Line 3 is repeated to form lines 9, 15, and 19. To write one, you have to have strong poetic lines, as we see in Dylan Thomas's famous villanelle.

Do Not Go Gentle Into That Good Night

Do not go gentle into that good night,
Old age should burn and rave at close of day;
Rage, rage against the dying of the light.

Though wise men at their end know dark is right,
Because their words had forked no lightning they
Do not go gentle into that good night.

Good men, the last wave by, crying how bright
Their frail deeds might have danced in a green bay,
Rage, rage against the dying of the light.

Wild men who caught and sang the sun in flight,
And learn, too late, they grieved it on its way,
Do not go gentle into that good night.

Grave men, near death, who see with blinding sight
Blind eyes could blaze like meteors and be gay,
Rage, rage against the dying of the light.

And you, my father, there on the sad height,
Curse, bless, me now with your fierce tears, I pray.
Do not go gentle into that good night.
Rage, rage against the dying of the light.

The sestina ("song of sixes") is a highly complex form tackled by poets who wish to try their skill. Six stanzas of six lines are followed by a three-line ENVOY. Six end words are used; these follow a fixed pattern requiring that all six words be used in each stanza—but they must be arranged differently each time. All the end words end up in the envoy! But even there, they follow a special order. Read W. H. Auden's sestina below that has as its subject the decay of cities. Perhaps all will be made clear—

Hearing of Harvests Rotting in the Valleys

Hearing of harvests rotting in the valleys,
Seeing at end of street the barren mountains,
Round corners coming suddenly on water,
Knowing them shipwrecked who were launched
for islands,
We honor founders of these starving cities,
Whose honor is the image of our sorrow.

Which cannot see its likeness in their sorrow
That brought them desperate to the brink of valleys;
Dreaming of evening walks through learned cities,
They reined their violent horses on the mountains,
Those fields like ships to castaways on islands,
Visions of green to them that craved for water,

They built by rivers and at night the water
Running past windows comforted their sorrow;
Each in his little bed conceived of islands
Where every day was dancing in the valleys,

And all the year trees blossomed on the mountains,
Where love was innocent, being far from cities.

But dawn came back and they were still in cities;
No marvellous creature rose up from the water,
There was still gold and silver in the mountains,
And hunger was a more immediate sorrow;
Although to moping villagers in valleys
Some waving pilgrims were describing islands.
"The gods," they promised, "visit us from islands,
Are stalking head-up, lovely through the cities;
Now is the time to leave your wretched valleys
And sail with them across the lime-green water;
Sitting at their white sides, forget their sorrow,
The shadow cast across your lives by mountains."

So many, doubtful, perished in the mountains
Climbing up crags to get a view of islands;
So many, fearful, took with them their sorrow
Which stayed them when they reached unhappy cities;
So many, careless, dived and drowned in water;
So many, wretched, would not leave their valleys.

It is the sorrow; shall it melt? Ah, water
Would gush, flush, green these mountains and
  these valleys
And we rebuild our cities, not dream of islands.

You may be wondering why such a difficult form should be included in a basic book like this. It's because as a writer you need to know the landscape, from the simplest haiku to the most complex sestina. Who knows? Maybe someday you'll want to climb the Mt. Everest or play the Rachmaninoff of poetry.

The last interlocking form we'll consider is the pantoum. It's not too difficult to write but does require skill and thought. This form, originally from Malaya, was brought to the West by Victor Hugo in 1829. Here's how it works. Write four lines of poetry. Fill them with imagery. Number the lines. In stanza two, repeat the lines according to this pattern: line 2 from the first stanza becomes line 1 in the second. Line 4 from the first becomes line 3 in the second. Lines 2 and 4 in this stanza are new ones you will write. The next stanza repeats the pattern. There's no limit to the number of stanzas in a pantoum, but let's simplify the form by thinking in terms of four.

When you come to the final stanza, all the lines are written. It is up to you to decide the order. Use lines 1 and 3 from the first stanza, and lines 2 and 4 from the third. Ending with line 1 gives the poem a strong finish, like a circle being closed.

Here's a pantoum written as an assignment by one of my seventh-grade students:

The First Snow of Winter

Snowflakes flutter down from the gray sky.
Quick and quiet, they fall on the dry ground.
Grass withers and dies under the heavy blanket.
The crows mournfully cry.

Quick and quiet, they fall on the dry ground.
Little feet leave boot prints in the snow.
The crows mournfully cry.
Trees droop, arms laden with snow.

Little feet leave boot prints in the snow.
Icicles shimmer like glass prisms.
Trees droop, arms laden with snow.
The first snow of winter has fallen.

Snowflakes flutter down from the gray sky.
Grass withers and dies under the heavy blanket.
Icicles shimmer like glass prisms.
The first snow of winter has fallen.

—Rachael Emery

I thought it would be fun to try one, so here's my attempt:

My Mother Smites the Sun

My mother is a tulip. She gets noticed.
She greets you with a strong red smile.
Lesser plants like periwinkles draw near.
The sun is smitten with her.

She greets you with a strong red smile.
Around her nothing stays wrong for long.
The sun is smitten with her.
She's listened to crickets and knows to sing.

Around her nothing stays wrong for long.
Death has often tried to close her cup.
She's listened to crickets and knows to sing.
Winter is coming. She'll hold her ground.

My mother is a tulip. She gets noticed.
Lesser plants like periwinkles draw near.
Death has often tried to close her cup.
Winter is coming. She'll hold her ground.

Now you try it.

The last fixed form we want to consider is Hebrew thought rhyme or parallelism. By this we mean two or more lines of poetry that say the same thing in two different ways. Parallelism adds literary power to poetry already richly figurative and sensuously detailed, as we see in such metaphors as blood crying from the ground or the sun being compared to a bridegroom coming out of his chamber. Leland Ryken, quoting a biblical scholar, offers a helpful explanation of parallelism in his book *Words of Delight*:

> It is clear that there is repetition in the parallel lines. But almost invariably something is added, and it is precisely the combination of what is repeated and what is added that makes of parallelism the artistic

> form that it is. The intimate relation between the old and new elements is an important feature of Hebrew composition and Hebrew thought. On the one hand we observe form and pattern; on the other form and pattern are radically altered.

In reading the Bible, awareness of parallelism as a literary structure can add to our appreciation of inspired poetry designed in such a way as to achieve balance, cadence, and grandeur. Four kinds of parallel structures appear in the Bible. The first is SYNONYMOUS. Two thoughts are essentially the same, but said differently:

> Your word is a lamp to my feet
> And a light to my path.
>
> (Ps. 119:105)

> The words of a man's mouth are deep waters;
> The wellspring of wisdom is a flowing brook.
>
> (Prov. 18:4)

Next is ANTITHETIC PARALLELISM. Here, the thoughts are contrasting:

> Righteousness exalts a nation,
> But sin is a reproach to any people.
>
> (Prov. 14:34)

> A wise son makes a glad father,
> But a foolish son is the grief of his mother.
>
> (Prov. 10:1)

A variation on this type is for the first line to make a positive statement and the second, to restate it negatively:

> The blessing of the Lord makes one rich,
> And He adds no sorrow with it.
>
> (Prov. 10:22)

Trust in the Lord with all your heart,
And lean not on your own understanding.

(Prov. 3:5)

CLIMACTIC PARALLELISM has a cumulative effect, with the second line repeating the first and adding to it:

Give unto the Lord, O you mighty ones,
Give unto the Lord glory and strength.

(Ps. 29:1)

Thy right hand, O Lord, glorious in power,
Thy right hand, O Lord, shatters the enemy.

(Exod. 15:6)

In SYNTHETIC PARALLELISM, the paired lines together form a complete thought. The second finishes the idea of the first but does not restate it.

You will guide me with Your counsel,
and afterward receive me to glory.

(Ps. 73:24)

He who answers a matter before he hears it,
It is folly and shame to him.

(Prov. 18:13)

Stepping Stones

Praise in Parallels

» Look in your Bible for examples of all four kinds of parallelisms. Write a prayer or a praise-poem to God experimenting with one or more of the different kinds.

Writing a formal poem is like filling a bathtub with water. The water fills and fits the shape. But writing free verse is like turning on a shower. The water rivets and runs as it will. There are some controls, of course. You can adjust the spray to be soft or hard, and bend the shower head high or low. The term free verse is unfortunate, suggesting that "anything goes." Actually, in the hands of an accomplished poet, the demands are just as great, though different, as those for closed form. Of course, it is true that much bad poetry has been written in the free verse school. But the same can be said for more traditional poetry.

Writing poems in open form involves a different set of challenges than for closed form. While the writer of the first doesn't have to worry about finding end words that rhyme or selecting words that fit a fixed meter, he does look for "the best words in the best order," as Coleridge defined poetry. This poet cares about sound and uses such things as assonance and consonance, internal rhyme, and rhythm. A great many of the poems written in open form seem quite traditional. They may be divided into stanzas. But again, a set metrical pattern versus a non-metrical one marks the dividing line between open and closed form.

Many writers of open form are anything but traditional. They may use white space creatively, leaving extra space

Stepping Stones

Playing with Space

» Write a poem that involves motion. Use white space to recreate the sense of that motion, placing the words of the poem in unconventional positions. For example, if you were to write about a slug, you might try:

```
treads a      sil-
                   ver
              trail.........
                             sl-
                                   ow go ing
s n a i l
r o a d . . .
```

» Playing around with words and white space is not a new innovation. Three hundred years ago, George Herbert was shaping poems to visually represent content and meaning. The most famous example is "Easter Wings," which we referred to in a previous chapter. You may want to do a bit of research on falconry before studying the poem—

Lord, who createdst man in wealth and store,
Though foolishly he lost the same,
Decaying more and more
Till he became
Most poor:
With thee
O let me rise
As larks, harmoniously,
And sing this day thy victories:
Then shall the fall further the flight in me.

My tender age in sorrow did begin:
And still with sicknesses and shame
Thou didst so punish sin,
That I became
Most thin.
With thee
Let me combine,
And feel this day thy victory;
For, if I imp my wing on thine,
Affliction shall advance the flight in me.

» Write a shaped poem with the Resurrection as your subject. Read the Gospel accounts for a fresh look. Take an object associated with Christ's passion and resurrection, such as the tomb or the cup, and write the poem, arranging the printed words accordingly.

between words and letters, arranging lines in unusual positions, or taking *out* space, as we saw earlier in E. E. Cummings' spring poem. Rather than following predetermined rules, the writer of free verse attends to the demands of the poem under construction.

9. Genres

When you sit down to write a poem, you make a number of decisions, whether consciously or subconsciously. Which word to put down first? Feather? Barnacle? So much depends on that word, those first words. "Of Man's First Disobedience, and the Fruit." Thus begins *Paradise Lost*, the great EPIC of English literature. Milton, following in Homer's footsteps, invokes the Muse at the poem's beginning—but it is no pagan goddess he addresses. "Sing Heav'nly Muse," he petitions, and identifies his Muse as the Spirit who inspired Moses. Such divine aid we need to write a poem: "Unless the Lord build the house, they labor in vain that build it."

How shall we build? Materials and structure we have considered in great detail in chapters on words, images, and form. But there is also the matter of the speaker. Who will tell the poem? And what will be the means of telling? What *kind* of poem will we write? We can classify a poem as being one of several types, or genres: LYRIC, NARRATIVE, EPIC, BALLAD, ELEGY, DRAMATIC MONOLOGUE, and DIDACTIC.

Lyric poetry is so named because of its original association with music. *Lyre* is from the Greek, meaning a stringed instrument of the harp family. In ancient Greek drama, a member of the chorus might step forward and deliver a song of deep feeling as he strummed the lyre. But with the invention of the printing press, poetry came to be enjoyed for its own sake—apart from music and singing. Yet the emphasis on feeling has remained. The lyric can be defined as a short poem that expresses personal feelings and thoughts in imaginative language.

He Wishes for the Cloths of Heaven

Had I the heavens' embroidered cloths,
Enwrought with golden and silver light,
The blue and the dim and the dark cloths
Of night and light and the half-light,
I would spread the cloths under your feet:
But I, being poor, have only my dreams;
I have spread my dreams under your feet;
Tread softly because you tread on my dreams.

—William Butler Yeats

Stepping Stones

Musical Rain

» Write in your journal on a rainy day. Record the sound and sight of rain, using a simile or two. Notice how the rain looks on different objects, how it sounds on the roof. How does the falling rain make you feel? Melancholy? Cozy and content? Write down all these impressions and more.

» Now write a lyric, selecting those images and metaphors you like best. Put them in an order that seems right to you. Infuse the poem with feeling, not by using words to describe your feelings, but by using suggestive imagery. Give your poem an imaginative title.

» Here's a lyric written by one of my students, Jeannie Imbody, when she was twelve. For this poem, she won first prize in a contest:

After the Rain

Strange how the rain changes things:
The spider web to a dainty lake,
Raindrops to clear bits of snow
Clinging to the woven surface,
The evergreen to a towering turret
Sparkling with hidden jewels,
Crystals ready to drop, yielding
To the fairy touch.
All is silent . . . and very still
(But for the bell-like "plink" of water
As a raindrop drips into a pool)
Awaiting the outcome of whispered debate
Between weather and wind and wood.
And then . . .
The sun shines through the rain,
Like a quavering smile through tears.

A poem that tells a story is a narrative. It may be simple and short or long and complex. "Stopping by Woods on a Snowy Evening" by Robert Frost is a short narrative poem familiar to many people (in fact, we quoted from it earlier):

Whose woods these are I think I know.
His house is in the village though;
He will not see me stopping here
To watch his woods fill up with snow.

My little horse must think it queer
To stop without a farmhouse near
Between the woods and frozen lake
The darkest evening of the year.

He gives his harness bells a shake
To ask if there is some mistake.
The only other sound's the sweep
Of easy wind and downy flake.

The woods are lovely, dark and deep,
But I have promises to keep,
And miles to go before I sleep,
And miles to go before I sleep.

Here we have all the elements of story: characters, plot, setting, point of view, theme. Who are the characters? What is the speaker's conflict? How is it resolved? What elements of setting are described?

You might enjoy reading some of Frost's longer narrative poems, such as *Death of the Hired Man* and *Home Burial*. These show great psychological insight into the characters, primarily through dialogue.

One of the best-loved long narrative poems in the English language is the *Rime of the Ancient Mariner* by Samuel Coleridge. Look for it in your library and read it if you like strangeness and thrilling adventure wrapped in a morality tale.

Stepping Stones

Sad Story-Poems

» A genuine artist does not balk at truth, no matter how disturbing. But there is something redemptive about the words themselves, the sad and beautiful words of tragic stories, that helps to lighten the load. Read the following narrative poem by Bruce Weigl, paying careful attention to the religious imagery, the overtones of war, and the speaker's poignant confession of his need of comfort. Write your response in your journal, then compose a narrative poem in which you tell a painful story of your own experience.

Shelter

I need some cover tonight from the dark.
I need some shelter from the wings
who beat my head into memory
where my sister sleeps

in the small upstairs bedroom
among the crucifixes and dried palm leaves,
among the lavender smell
of our grandmother's
Sunday black silk dress
in her house where we've come as a family
after church,
the brothers of Belgrade
and the wives from across the river
which is called the river of blood.

In the crowded kitchen,
below my sleeping sister
a beautiful dandelion salad
waits like a bouquet
with blood sausage on a plate
and black bread and dark wine
and the aunts and uncles
and their children in their orbits
and the language
rough and thick on my tongue
when I try to say the words
because the air is suddenly wronged.

My grandfather swears too loud.
His brothers only laugh.
The women shush them all, Eat,
eat they say across the room
but something's cut too deep this time
and the children are pushed
with grace towards the porch and backyard,

and from behind the tree of drunken plums
I watch my grandfather
wave his pistol in the air
and his brothers reach for it
as in a frieze
and the shot explodes
through the low ceiling
through the bedroom floor
where my sister sleeps and lives on.
I need some shelter tonight.
I need the sleeping hands to waken once again.

A story that is sung is called a BALLAD. Look in your library for recordings of "Bonny Barbara Allen," "Sir Patrick Spence," "Edward," "John Henry," "The Twa Corbies," "The Cruel Mother," and others. Tales of love, betrayal, and revenge are typical. Ballads are anonymous, handed down through many generations and sung across oceans.

A special kind of narrative poem, one seldom written today (probably because of the more popular movies like *Star Wars!*) is the epic, a long narrative featuring a hero (or heroes) who does brave exploits and undergoes exciting adventures. The hero is a figure of national or international importance, one who stands out in history. The epic style of poetry is grand and elevated. Supernatural powers get involved in the action. The setting covers a wide range, even the whole earth or universe.

Famous epics are the *Iliad,* the *Odyssey, Beowulf,* the *Song of Roland*, the *Aeneid,* and *Paradise Lost.* Dante's *Divine Comedy* is classified as an epic although it lacks a number of the characteristics mentioned.

The ELEGY is a sad, pensive poem or lament. It is also the name given a poem written on the occasion of someone's death. If you read the major writers of centuries past, you find a considerable number of elegies written for children who died in infancy and youth. It is sobering to reflect on the fact that before our modern age, losing children to incurable illness and disease was commonplace. Cotton Mather, for example, a minister and historian of Puritan New England, lost thirteen of his fifteen children before he died. Below is an elegy by Anne Bradstreet on the death of her month-old grandchild, Simon. Notice that three children from this family are gone:

> No sooner came, but gone, and fall'n asleep.
> Acquaintance short, yet parting caused us weep;
> Three flowers, two scarcely blown, the last i' th' bud,
> Cropped by th' Almighty's hand; yet is He good.

With dreadful awe before Him let's be mute,
Such was His will, but why, let's not dispute,
With humble hearts and mouths put in the dust,
Let's say He's merciful as well as just.
He will return and make up all our losses,
And smile again after our bitter crosses
Go pretty babe, go rest with sisters twain
Among the blessed in endless joys remain.

Here's a moving elegy by A. E. Housman.

To an Athlete Dying Young

The time you won your town the race
We chaired you through the market-place;
Man and boy stood cheering by,
And home we brought you shoulder-high.

Today, the road all runners come,
Shoulder-high we bring you home,
And set you at your threshold down,
Townsman of a stiller town.

Smart lad, to slip betimes away
From fields where glory does not stay,
And early though the laurel grows
It withers quicker than the rose.

Eyes the shady night has shut
Cannot see the record cut,
And silence sounds no worse than cheers
After earth has stopped the ears.

Now you will not swell the rout
Of lads that wore their honors out,
Runners whom renown outran
And the name died before the man.

So set, before its echoes fade,
The fleet foot on the sill of shade,
And hold to the low lintel up
The still-defended challenge-cup.
And round that early-laureled head

Will flock to gaze the strengthless dead,
And find unwithered on its curls
The garland briefer than a girl's.

How does the poet achieve the sorrowful tone? Which images do you think are especially poignant? What is the poem's major contrast?

Stepping Stones

Writing an Elegy

» Read "Names of Horses" by Donald Hall in the "Gathering of Poems" section. Think about a deceased pet or farm animal that has served you faithfully. Write down descriptions of the animal. Brainstorm ways the animal has been a blessing to you and your family. Now write an elegy commemorating the beast. Be sure your poem contains sufficient imagery.

A DRAMATIC MONOLOGUE is similar to a SOLILOQUY, the latter being a speech delivered by a character in a play who is alone and allows the audience or reader to know his thoughts. Here we think of Hamlet puzzling over whether "To be or not to be." But there is more to the dramatic monologue, for though we hear conversation of a single character, it is a speech that comes at some moment of reckoning in the speaker's life. A second distinguishing feature is that the speaker is not thinking out loud, as with soliloquy, but is speaking in the presence of a silent listener. The most famous example is "My Last Duchess" by the Victorian poet Robert Browning, who is credited with creating the dramatic monologue. Browning developed characters whose words reveal them to be wicked, weak, mad, or proud. In "My Last Duchess," which takes place in Ferrara, Italy, the speaker is a jealous, proud, controlling man. What sort of woman was his late wife? Fra Pandolf and Claus of Innsbruck are the names of artists Browning has invented for the poem—

My Last Duchess

Ferrara
That's my last Duchess painted on the wall,
Looking as if she were alive. I call
That piece a wonder, now; Fra Pandolf's hands
Worked busily a day, and there she stands.
Will't please you sit and look at her? I said
"Fra Pandolf" by design, for never read
Strangers like you that pictured countenance,
The depth and passion of its earnest glance,
But to myself they turned (since none puts by
The curtain I have drawn for you, but I)
And seemed as they would ask me, if they durst,
How such a glance came there; so, not the first
Are you to turn and ask thus. Sir, 'twas not
Her husband's presence only, called that spot
Of joy into the Duchess' cheek; perhaps
Fra Pandolf chanced to say, "Her mantle laps
Over my lady's wrist too much," or "Paint
Must never hope to reproduce the faint
Half-flush that dies along her throat." Such stuff
Was courtesy, she thought, and cause enough
For calling up that spot of joy. She had
A heart—how shall I say?—too soon made glad,
Too easily impressed; she liked whate'er
She looked on, and her looks went everywhere.
Sir, 'twas all one! My favor at her breast,
The dropping of the daylight in the West,
The bough of cherries some officious fool
Broke in the orchard for her, the white mule
She rode with round the terrace—all and each
Would draw from her alike the approving speech,
Or blush, at least. She thanked men,—good! but thanked
Somehow I know not how as if she ranked
My gift of a nine-hundred-years-old name
With anybody's gift. Who'd stoop to blame
This sort of trifling? Even had your skill
In speech—which I have not—to make your will

Quite clear to such an one, and say "Just this
Or that in you disgusts me; here you miss,
Or there exceed the mark"—and if she let
Herself be lessoned so, nor plainly set
Her wits to yours, forsooth, and made excuse—
E'en then would be some stooping; and I choose
Never to stoop. Oh, sir, she smiled, no doubt,
Whene'er I passed her; but who passed without
Much the same smile? This grew; I gave commands;
Then all smiles stopped together. There she stands
As if alive. Will't please you rise? We'll meet
The company below, then. I repeat,
The Count your master's known munificence
Is ample warrant that no just pretense
Of mine for dowry will be disallowed;
Though his fair daughter's self, as I avowed
At starting, is my object. Nay, we'll go
Together down, sir. Notice Neptune, though,
Taming a sea-horse, thought a rarity,
Which Claus of Innsbruck cast in bronze for me!

Stepping Stones

» Invent a negative character. Tell all about him or her in your journal, including name, age, descriptions of the character's appearance, likes, dislikes, home life—everything you can imagine to make the character come alive for you. Above all, think of your character as being mean or dishonest or stingy or cruel, one who even may remind you of someone you actually know. Now plan your dramatic monologue. (You may want to read a few other examples before you begin the poem. Robert Frost, Edwin Arlington Robinson, and Ezra Pound have written successfully in this genre.) Who will the character be speaking to? What is the setting? What is the decisive moment your character faces? Write the poem as a one-sided conversation. No narration is allowed. The speech must subtly reveal the character's flaws. A good strategy is to make the character seem outwardly one way—charming, perhaps, or religious—but inwardly spiteful or hard-hearted.

It has been said that all poetry instructs, but poems that instruct *explicitly* are DIDACTIC. These are poems that have a lesson to impart. Much didactic poetry isn't poetry at all, but mere verse, as in the *New England Primer*: "In Adam's fall, we sinn'd all." When the lesson is more important than the literary effect, the poem is something other than art. But happy is the poet whose words are apples of gold, whose passionate truth is a silver frame—

To a Waterfowl

Whither, 'midst falling dew,
While glow the heavens with the last steps of day,
Far, through their rosy depths, dost thou pursue
Thy solitary way?

Vainly the fowler's eye
Might mark thy distant flight to do thee wrong,
As, darkly seen against the crimson sky,
Thy figure floats along.

Seek'st thou the plashy brink
Of weedy lake, or marge of river wide,
Or where the rocking billows rise and sink
On the chafed ocean side?

There is a Power whose care
Teaches thy way along that pathless coast—
The desert and illimitable air—
Lone wandering, but not lost.

All day thy wings have fanned,
At that far height, the cold, thin atmosphere,
Yet stoop not, weary, to the welcome land,
Though the dark night is near.
And soon that toil shall end;
Soon shalt thou find a summer home, and rest,
And scream among thy fellows; reeds shall bend,
Soon, o'er thy sheltered nest.

Thou'rt gone, the abyss of heaven
Hath swallowed up thy form; yet, on my heart
Deeply has sunk the lesson thou hast given,
And shall not soon depart.

He who, from zone to zone,
Guides through the boundless sky thy certain flight,
In the long way that I must tread alone,
Will lead my steps aright.

—William Cullen Bryant

What lesson has the speaker learned?

In "The World Is Too Much with Us" by William Wordsworth, we see a Romantic ideal regarding nature and materialism. State the message in your own words—

The world is too much with us; late and soon,
Getting and spending, we lay waste our powers;
Little we see in Nature that is ours;
We have given our hearts away, a sordid boon!
This sea that bares her bosom to the moon;
The winds that will be howling at all hours,
And are up-gathered now like sleeping flowers;
For this, for everything, we are out of tune;
It moves us not. Great God! I'd rather be
A Pagan suckled in a creed outworn;
So might I, standing on this pleasant lea,
Have glimpses that would make me less forlorn;
Have sight of Proteus rising from the sea;
Or hear old Triton blow his wreathèd horn.

There are other poetic types, such as the PASTORAL, the AUBADE, and the EPIGRAM. We will omit discussion of these, but you can find their definitions in the glossary. Hopefully, this study of genres has opened up many new possibilities for you in your pursuit of poetry.

Stepping Stones

» List in your journal some issues you feel strongly about and your beliefs concerning them. Write a poem about one of them, but let the idea be triggered by an image or scene. For example, if you saw a junky old car with trash and french fries spilled all over the floor, it might remind you of the cheap, empty lives of many Americans. Think of your poem as a protest.

10. "Sing Darker"

Matters of Voice

When reading poetry, it is important to keep in mind that the poet and the speaker of the poem are not necessarily the same. In fact, they seldom are. Certainly some poems, like Milton's "When I Consider How My Light Is Spent" and Thomas's "Do Not Go Gentle into That Good Night," are autobiographical. But poets create fictitious characters called PERSONAE (the Greek word for mask) as in Tennyson's "Ulysses" to expand their vision. Often, a poem will have autobiographical elements, such as "Fern Hill." But in that poem, the speaker, like the farm itself, is idealized, and we hear his universal voice lamenting time and change and loss.

As you write poetry, try adopting other points of view. Imagine being a flea on a dog's back, a sole on a shoe, a figure in a stained glass panel.

Stepping Stones

Long-Ago Letters

» In the last chapter, you created an imaginary character for a dramatic monologue. Now take a historic figure you have studied and found interesting. Write a letter-poem in this person's voice. Leave off the greeting and salutation.

Or write a song. You can also do this with a character from literature whose point of view you would like to widen and deepen. Once, after teaching Shakespeare's *King Lear* to a college literature class, I wrote "Lear's Song," which a student put to music and performed with his band.

A famous opera singer was interviewed about her career. Encouraged to become a mezzo-soprano, she was told to "sing darker." Our emotional response to a work of art is influenced by what is called TONE. Is the voice in the poem sad, angry, amused, approving, cynical, sassy? Is the point of view ironic—that is, as we saw previously, do we the readers know more about the speaker (or situation) than he knows about himself? Ozymandias, the pharaoh in Shelley's poem, thought he was invincible. His might, embodied in great structures of stone, was in reality an illusion, for he died and all his works returned to sand. Thus, "Look on me, ye mighty and despair" is ironic because while Pharaoh intended his words to be intimidating to his subjects and enemies, we read *despair* differently. Proud, cruel tyrants should indeed despair, seeing in broken monuments their own destruction.

When you read a poem, consider carefully this matter of tone, sometimes called ATTITUDE. How would you describe the attitude of the speaker of the following poem, written by a college student for one of my classes?

King Fish

As far as fish go, I'm tops.
True, I spend hours preening
My salmon-gray mohawk,
As well as my tail—
But what fish *my* age doesn't?

It is going to be spawning season soon.
I've got to look good for the ladies.

Who could resist these dark
And ever-so-earnest eyes?

These strong, sensuous fins?
They don't come easy either.
You try swimming against the current all the time.

You may be wondering why
My chin is a little bloody.
Carp's gotta know what is,
And what isn't his rock.

Some say I don't smile enough—
Always got this serious look on my face.
But I do smile,
In the right company.

Yep.
When I smile
Everything smiles back.

If you'll excuse me,
I see a worm over there
With my name on it.

—Rachel LeBeau

One thing that influences tone is DICTION, or word choices. Does the writer use elevated language or a plain speaking tone of voice? Overall, we use the word STYLE to describe the manner in which the poem is written. Recall that in a previous chapter, we said that *poetic diction* is to be avoided on grounds it is artificial and archaic. When you write a poem, consider T. S. Eliot's advice in his essay "The Music of Poetry": "Poetry must not stray too far from the ordinary, everyday language that we use and hear." But within that range, poets compose in a variety of styles depending on their subject and purpose. Read the following two selections. Quite apart from subject matter, which is very different in each, how do they differ in style and tone?

Any Morning

Just lying on the couch and being happy.
Only humming a little, the quiet sound in the head.
Trouble is busy elsewhere at the moment, it has
so much to do in the world.

People who might judge are mostly asleep; they can't
monitor you all the time, and sometimes they forget.
When dawn flows over the hedge you can
get up and act busy.

Little corners like this, pieces of Heaven
left lying around, can be picked up and saved.
People won't even see that you have them,
they are so light and easy to hide.

Later in the day you can act like the others.
You can shake your head. You can frown.

—William Stafford

Dover Beach

The sea is calm to-night.
The tide is full, the moon lies fair
Upon the straits; on the French coast, the light
Gleams and is gone; the cliffs of England stand,
Glimmering and vast, out in the tranquil bay.
Come to the window, sweet is the night-air!

Only, from the long line of spray
Where the sea meets the moon-blanched land,
Listen! you hear the grating roar
Of pebbles which the waves draw back, and fling,
At their return, up the high strand,
Begin and cease, and then again begin,
With tremulous cadence slow, and bring
The eternal note of sadness in.
Sophocles long ago
Heard it on the Aegean, and it brought

Into his mind the turbid ebb and flow
Of human misery: we
Find also in the sound a thought,
Hearing it by this distant northern sea.

The sea of faith
Was once, too, at the full, and round earth's shore
Lay like the folds of a bright girdle furled.
But now I only hear
Its melancholy, long, withdrawing roar,
Retreating, to the breath
Of the night-wind, down the vast edges drear
And naked shingles of the world.

Ah, love, let us be true
To one another, for the world, which seems
To lie before us like a land of dreams,
So various, so beautiful, so new,
Hath really neither joy, nor love, nor light,
Nor certitude, nor peace, nor help for pain;
And we are here as on a darkling plain
Swept with confused alarms of struggle and flight,
Where ignorant armies clash by night.

—Matthew Arnold

In the first poem, the diction sounds like conversation, as if the speaker is talking to himself. The tone is light and charming, but the idea has weight, having to do with people who take life too seriously and resent those who take time out to do nothing for the sheer joy of it. In the second, the writing style is more formal and elevated with the use of classical allusion. The tone is dark and somber, reflecting a sense of futility felt by the speaker, a skeptic who concludes that in the modern world the only "truth" is found in love between two people.

Stepping Stones

» Read the poem below by James Still, a famous Appalachian writer. Write a brief analysis of its tone and diction.

Heritage

I shall not leave these prisoning hills
Though they topple their barren heads to level earth
And the forests slide uprooted out of the sky.
Though the waters of Troublesome, of Trace Fork,
Of Sand Lick rise in a single body to glean the valleys,
To drown lush pennyroyal, to unravel rail fences;
Though the sun-ball breaks the ridges into dust
And burns its strength into the blistered rock
I cannot leave. I cannot go away.

Being of these hills, being one with the fox
Stealing into the shadows, one with the new-born foal,
The lumbering ox drawing green beech logs to mill,
One with the destined feet of man climbing and
descending,
And one with death rising to bloom again, I cannot go.
Being of these hills I cannot pass beyond.

» Write a poem adopting the speaking tones and expressions of a person from a different background than yours—a street person, for example, or a farm hand. No stereotyping, please!

» Write a poem with an angry tone or a sad or cynical tone from the point of view of a person who has suffered loss.

» Write a poem in which you argue with yourself as if you were two people in one.

11. Writing, Reading, and Revising

Writing a poem demands intense concentration. What you are trying to do is match the weight of your feeling with words—kind of like stepping up on the doctor's scale and having the nurse push metal weights around until the scale's arm hangs in mid-air, perfectly balanced. The poet's province is experience, and precision of language is the way you convey it. You want others to taste cotton candy at the fair just as it seemed to you. You want them to feel your horror when you awoke in your tent and saw a wood spider the size of a hand. Think of an experience you enjoyed immensely. Think of the memory itself. It is more than a series of images in your mind. It is more than the go-kart, the bonfire, the cat in the window. Memory is the halo, the shadow: "Not the rose but the scent of the rose; not the sea, but the sound of the sea," as Eleanor Farjeon expressed it. The sense we have of something, the way it tugs at our heart or terrifies or amuses us—this is the material harvested by poets, who want words for their fun or grief. For fear, "zero at the bone." For love, "two hearts beating each to each."

Your journal is a key to getting at this inner world which is all the time speaking to us, if we would but listen. The journal is a listening device, an extra pair of eyes, a set of antennae. Develop a habit of jotting down impressions. Write down interesting words. Jack London, the author of *Call of the Wild* and other adventure novels, used to write new vocabulary words on note cards and string them around in his apartment to study and practice saying until they became part of his own speech. Emily Dickinson carried a dictionary around with her everywhere.

When you find a shapely sentence in your reading, write it in your journal. "The nights were comfortless and chill, and they did not dare to sing or talk too loud, for the echoes were uncanny, and the silence seemed to dislike being broken—except by the noise of water and the wail of wind and the crack of stone" (from *The Hobbit*). I also write down quotations that seem to me wise—"He that defines the words defines the world"; "How we spend our days is how we spend our lives"—and memorable phrases and expressions: "I pine for you, I balsalm" (from *Stuart Little*); "The wind had blown off, leaving a loud bright night with wings beating in the trees and a persistent organ sound as the full bellows of the earth blew the frogs full of life" (from *The Great Gatsby*). This is what a journal is: a sourcebook for poems (and songs, stories, plays, essays, ideas for a novel).

To write you must read. Many good books. Many poems. Dare I say, to *live* you must read. "Man shall not live by bread alone but by every word that proceedeth out of the mouth of the Father." God makes Himself known through language. This is why the decline of literacy in our nation is so disturbing. People who can't or don't read sink into a deadly swamp of mind, ignorant of God, history, beauty, themselves, of how the world can be.

I suggest you start with an anthology of poems by recognized poets, many of whom have been mentioned in this book. Sample different styles and subjects, past and present. Then check out entire collections—the works of

Theodore Roethke or George Herbert or Elizabeth Bishop, so as to become better acquainted with their writing. Poetry is not easily read. It requires slow absorption. Because it is condensed, imaginative language, you must do some work to comprehend it. First, read the poem aloud, then silently several times. Ask yourself these questions:

1. What is the situation of the poem? (It helps if you paraphrase it.)
2. Who is the speaker (or speakers)?
3. Are there words whose meanings you don't know? Look them up in the dictionary. Are there ALLUSIONS, that is, references to events, characters, and ideas from history, the Bible and other literature? Be sure to look these up as well.
4. What is the tone? What kind of diction is used?
5. How is the poem to be classified (lyric, dramatic monologue, narrative, etc.)? Closed or open form? If closed, what rhyme scheme and meter?
6. What sounds are prominent? What does sound reveal about sense?
7. What images are prominent? What figures of speech?
8. What oppositions can I find in the poem? For example, do I find contrasting images, as in "When Icicles Hang by the Wall" (page 86) with its opposition of harsh winter and the comforts of companionship within the village? Is the speaker struggling with a moral issue that clashes with another principle? Is there a conflict between flesh and spirit, nature and science, war and peace, desire and restraint?
9. Is the poem playful or serious? Or both?
10. What vision or theme is conveyed? For example, in the "Lake Isle of Innisfree," the narrator imagines a cabin he dreams of building at Innisfree, and these dreams enable him to survive the gray pavements of everyday existence.

Thus, the poem is about the imaginative life and the need we all have at times for escape.

11. What is the significance of the title?

12. What do you think was the poet's purpose? How well did he or she achieve it?

Stepping Stones

Something Fishy

» Read and study the following poem, then write answers to the questions above. (Hint: The next-to-last line of the poem is an allusion.)

The Fish

I caught a tremendous fish
and held him beside the boat
half out of water, with my hook
fast in a corner of his mouth.
He didn't fight.
He hadn't fought at all.
He hung a grunting weight,
battered and venerable
and homely. Here and there
his brown skin hung in strips
like ancient wall-paper,
and its pattern of darker brown
was like wall-paper:
shapes like full-blown roses
stained and lost through age.
He was speckled with barnacles,
fine rosettes of lime,
and infested
with tiny white sea-lice,
and underneath two or three
rags of green weed hung down.
While his gills were breathing in
the terrible oxygen
—the frightening gills,
fresh and crisp with blood,
that can cut so badly—I thought of
the coarse white flesh
packed in like feathers,

the big bones and the little bones,
the dramatic reds and blacks
of his shiny entrails,
and the pink swim-bladder
like a big peony.

I looked into his eyes
which were far larger than mine
but shallower, and yellowed,
the irises backed and packed
with tarnished tinfoil
seen through the lenses
of old scratched isinglass.
They shifted a little, but not
to return my stare.
—It was more like the tipping
of an object toward the light.
I admired his sullen face,
the mechanism of his jaw,
and then I saw
that from his lower lip
—if you could call it a lip—
grim, wet, and weapon-like,
hung five old pieces of fish-line,
or four and a wire leader
with the swivel still attached,
with all their five big hooks
grown firmly in his mouth.
A green line, frayed at the end
where he broke it, two heavier lines,
and a fine black thread
still crimped from the strain and snap
when it broke and he got away.
Like medals with their ribbons frayed
  and wavering,
a five-haired beard of wisdom
trailing from his aching jaw.
I stared and stared
and victory filled up
the little rented boat,
from the pool of bilge
where oil had spread a rainbow
around the rusted engine
to the bailer rusted orange,

> the sun-cracked thwarts,
> the oarlocks on their strings,
> the gunnels—until everything
> was rainbow, rainbow, rainbow!
> And I let the fish go.
>
> —Elizabeth Bishop

Now we come to the business of writing the poem. When thinking of subjects, stop and think about what fascinates you—odd things, like motels from the fifties and semi-trucks, Muscovy ducks and sea glass. In her book *The Writing Life,* Annie Dillard asserts that our true subjects lie in "that idiosyncratic thought you advert to." She goes on to say, "There is something you find interesting, for a reason hard to explain. It is hard to explain because you have never read it on any page; there you begin. You were made and set here to give voice to this, your own astonishment."

I love this phrase: *your own astonishment*. It is entirely biblical. "There be three things which are too wonderful for me," cried Agur the son of Jakeh, "yea, four which I know not: the way of an eagle in the air; the way of a serpent upon a rock; the way of a ship in the midst of the sea; and the way of a man with a maid" (Prov. 30:18–19).

Make a list of astonishing things. Think 'way back to when you were small. What fascinated you then? What fascinates you now? Remember, too, that the best sources for poems are words, experiences, objects, dreams, and ideas from books that evoke strong emotion.

It is always a good idea to write in your journal before you compose the actual poem. In my various notebooks are phrases and ideas for poems. Here's a sampling. *A deer racing along a fence by a highway, looking for an entrance back into the wilderness. A big white circle in the lawn where Emily's pool was (looks like a face). Rock cliffs in winter are wizards, bearded with ice. Horse gate, Broad Wall, Fountain Gate, Fish Gate, Dung Gate, Old Gate, Valley Gate, Tower of the Furnaces, Pool of Siloam, Dragon's Well, King's Pool, Water Gate, Sheep Gate, East Gate, Muster Gate.*

An important principle to keep in mind as you write is the lesson of Moses' rod. Take as your subject what's right under your nose and expect a transformation. In Old Testament (Exod. 4), God asked Moses, "What is that in your hand?" Moses answered, "A rod." Then the Lord told him to "Cast it on the ground." When Moses did this, the Bible tells us that the rod became a serpent and that "Moses fled from it." God's touch is powerful. We know not what He will bring to life. "Reach out your hand and take it by the tail," He commanded Moses, who obeyed and found the serpent turned back into a rod.

While the text primarily concerns God's miraculous dealings with His servant and His people, I don't think it inappropriate to consider the rod and the serpent as symbols for God's transforming power as applied to the imagination. Ordinary experience—the kneading of bread, the polishing of an apple—becomes sanctified and altered. The Puritan poet and minister Edward Taylor recognized that his art depended on God's grace, saying that even if his pen were "an angel's quill"

> And sharpened on a precious stone ground tight,
> And dipped in liquid gold, and moved by skill
> In Crystal leaves should golden letters write,
> It would but blot and blur, yea, jag and jar
> Unless thou mak'st the pen, and scrivener.[1]

Write the poem for glory—not your own but God's. Pray for His aid. Remember, you are yourself a poem,

[1] scrivener: *scribe*

God's handiwork. (When my children were little, they sang a song from Bible school—"The mountains are His, the rivers are His, the stars are His *dandiwork,* too." We loved that word and never told them any different!) Let words and phrases flow. Seek fresh, strong imagery. Include metaphors, similes and other figures of speech. Listen to the music in your head and move with it. If you establish a meter, stay mostly with it. Occasionally, break your meter, to add variety and interest. When you write, give of yourself—"Freely you have received. Freely give." From Dillard: "Spend it all, shoot it, play it, lose it, all, right away, every time." Don't hold back. Don't edit, not yet. Like Whitman, load your lines with details. Like Frost, tell a small story. Like Dickinson, find striking similes. Like Hopkins, find internal rhyme. Learn from the great writers. But be yourself. Say the truest thing you know, line by line.

After you've produced a draft and worked it into a shape you're fairly pleased with, get your pen-knife out and start cutting. Delete careless repetitions and wordiness, as in the following first draft by student Emily Windes:

Potato

A potato is rough, brown, and wrinkled,
It's lined and wrinkled like an old man's face,
The skin looks like dirt or an elephant's skin
It sprouts, it looks like little trees are growing out of the
dirty skin.
The sprouts are green, with hairs and bumps.
A sprouting potato looks like an animal with crazy legs.

Here's her final draft:

Potato

The potato—rough, brown and wrinkled,
Lined like an old man's face.
The skin looks like dirt or an elephant's hide.

It sprouts little trees with hairs and bumps.
A sprouting potato is like an animal with crazy legs.

What changes did she make? What words did she eliminate or find synonyms for? Notice, too, that the basic poem was there, in the first draft, like a face in a slab of marble. The sculptor must chisel away the stone that is *not* the face. The writer must cut out words that are not the poem.

Below is another poem, followed by a revision, both written by student Chris Greene when he was ten. The assignment was to take a walk in the woods in the fall and write a poem using language appealing to all five senses. I also asked the class to include a metaphor or simile—

The Way God Made It

I walk along, my head up high,
And see a robin flapping by,
It says "tweet tweet" and that's just fine
'Cause that's the way God made it.
I see a squirrel scamper by,
It scurries up a tree,
And that's just fine
'Cause that's the way God made it.
I look back up, the birdie's gone
I look back down upon the ground
and I thank God I'm safe and sound.

The night before class, Chris called me on the phone saying he wasn't very happy with his poem (neither was I!) and that he was trying to revise it. He said he couldn't think of any metaphors to include. I said, "Chris, did you really take a walk in the woods?" He admitted that he had not. (No wonder the poem lacks verisimilitude!) I asked, "Do you ever go on walks?" He said yes, he walks around in his neighborhood. So I asked him to tell me about it. What do you see? People, he said. What people? I asked. What are their names? And he mentioned Mr. Pope. What else do you see? He said squirrels. I told him *scamper* is what everyone says about squirrels. Think again. What does its movement remind you of? And so he wrote the revision, which follows. Notice how much more convincing it is. Notice the wonderfully imaginative simile describing the squirrel. Notice the sense of closure.

A Walk in My Neighborhood

I went on a walk in my neighborhood.
Crickets in the grass chirped big and bold.
I said "howdy" to Mr. Pope
And he waved back to me.
The squirrel ran down the tree
Like water out of a faucet.
My best friend Brian went riding by,
Going to choir practice.
As I got to a big oak tree
I thought I might climb to the top
And see sidewalks like streams
And people coming home from busy days.

I've given these two actual examples to show you the kinds of revisions you make when you create poetry.

Here are a few additional suggestions. Give thought to your title. Sometimes it's good to pull a catchy phrase out of the poem to use as your title. Sometimes your title will give crucial information not included in the poem proper. A title can be simple and straightforward, but it should always shed light on the poem's meaning and be in keeping with its tone.

As much as possible, avoid the verb *to be* and all its forms: is, are, was, were. Use strong verbs instead, as discussed in chapter two.

After you've written the poem, try omitting the first couple of lines. Often the first thing we write is mere scaffolding, a vantage point from which to write. It can easily be eliminated with no loss to the poem. Try moving things around. The ending might be your true beginning.

Take special care with the last word of a line, for it occupies a weighty position. If you have a long line that carries over into the next space, indent it. Otherwise, break lines in logical places, as with a pause or end. Sometimes—say, to create a jolting, jarring motion—a poet will break lines at odd moments. The best way to learn the skill of lineation is to read a great deal of poetry and to experiment with different effects.

Stepping Stones

Extreme Words

» Here's a project you can do in your journal over a period of time. Make a list of 75 verbs with extreme sounds: glug, trudge, drizzle, stumble. Use your dictionary. Draw from this list when you write. Make a list of 75 nifty nouns: pomade, unction, dalliance, labyrinth. Use this list, too.

Closed for Remodeling

» Revise the following poem, adding imagery, omitting verbiage (word garbage), improving sound and sense.

Night Magic

In the still of the night
while I am reading a book,
the old house settles.
Beyond the windows,
the lawn is full of shadows.
The shadows dance in the pale moonlight.
Beyond the shadows
the alley has its own sounds
and sights.
Beyond the alley
is the rest of the world
which I visit
in books and dreams.

Aim for freshness and originality. If you've heard a phrase or metaphor before, don't use it.

Beware of stating the obvious or summing up your poem for the reader. End with an image, not a lecture.

Helps for Writing and Revising

1. Every word must earn its keep. Weak, trite, out-of-place words must go.

2. Remember curtains and windows. If you use an abstraction or state a generalization (window), be sure to pull the curtains back to reveal details and images.

3. Thicken the gravy. Choose words for their connotative value. Go for more meaning.

4. Use figurative language.

5. Have fun with words.

6. When revising, always ask yourself, "what if?" This opens up new ways of thinking about your poem. What if I moved the lines around? What if I got rid of these words or that phrase? What if I changed the title?

7. If you follow a meter, be consistent. But every now and then, throw in a bump or curve.

8. Avoid careless repetitions of words and phrases. On the other hand, you may wish to use repetition for literary effect.

9. Choose words for their sounds and rhythms as well as meaning. If you are aiming for smoothness, you probably wouldn't want a hard-edged, polysyllabic word like "regimentation."

10. If you use rhymes, try mixing in slant rhymes.

11. Name things: streets, people, cafes.

12. Include colors.

13. Write phrases and fragments when you need to. Don't think you have to write in complete sentences. Remember, you are writing poetry, not paragraphs.

14. Include a surprise in your poem—some striking phrase or unexpected detail. Think of your poem as being like a box of Crackerjacks!

15. Type up your poem. Arrange lines in suitable fashion. Proofread carefully for misspelled words and faulty grammar and usage.

16. After you've written the poem, put it away and forget about it for a couple of weeks. Then go back to it with a fresh, clear eye.

17. Compose a thoughtful, captivating title.

At some point, you will look at your poem, this loaf of words that you've beaten and kneaded and shaped and baked, and be able to say, "Finished." You're pleased with your final product. You think you'll be writing many poems. Because writing is a public as well as a private activity, it's good to think about reaching an audience. This is the publishing aspect of writing.

Publishing may take the form of typing your poem in a cool font, printing it out on card stock, framing it, and presenting it to your dad as a gift. It can mean submitting poems to a school newspaper, a contest, or a magazine. It involves the recognition that in a sense our poems do not belong to us, any more than our talents do. True, Emily Dickinson hid her poems in drawers and Minister Edward Taylor forbade his descendants to publish his poems, written for an audience of One. But the drawers and vault were opened; the words saw light. Because that is the nature of words.

How do you go about finding contests and magazines that publish poetry of young people? If you attend a traditional school, ask your English teacher. The Internet is a good source of information, with poetry sites in abundance. Use your search engine to find "children's poetry contests." Enter "National Scholastic Awards" for information about one of the most distinguished sponsors of writing and art awards. Call your local newspaper to ask about local and regional contests. In our area, southwest Virginia and east Tennessee, a festival is held each summer which sponsors a creative writing contest open to anyone. Many of my students have won cash prizes for poems and stories.

If you wish to submit your work to be published in a magazine, you might want to buy a copy of *The Market Guide for Young Writers*. The book is for writers ages 8–18 and includes over 150 markets and contests. Find out more by viewing the Writer's Market Internet site (www.writersdigest.com). Typically, market manuals give alphabetical listings of magazines and journals with descriptions of what editors are looking for, guidelines for submission, payment, etc.

Preparing your manuscript is an art in itself. Type your name, address, and telephone number in the upper left or right-hand corner. Type each poem on a separate page with the title centered above it. Should you double or single-space the lines? Editors have different preferences. I usually single-space my poems. Make sure you have no misspelled words or punctuation errors. Use good bond paper and make sure it's white. It should be standard size (8½ x 11"). The printed copy should be neat, with no smudges or bent corners.

Submit three to six poems at a time. Tri-fold the manuscript to fit inside a white business envelope. Address it to the editor (make sure you spell his or her name correctly!), then write the name and address of the publication. Enclose a self-addressed, stamped envelope in with your poems. (You can fold this in thirds, too.) Drop it in the slot. Pray. Then try to forget you did any of this. Otherwise, you will find yourself listening for the mail carrier's footsteps every day and engaging in hand-to-hand combat with anyone who dares try to get the mail before you do.

Eventually, the envelope will come back. Most likely there will be a form letter saying, "Sorry," along with your three folded poems looking deflated and forlorn. But there may come a day when the envelope comes with good news. You've won the contest. Or your poem has been accepted for publication. You'll whoop and holler and dance around the house. This heart-breaking, heart-warming process of publishing is valuable, for it improves both poet and poem by making the writer tough and by setting high standards. Even more gratifying is the day the magazine arrives in the mail with your poem and your name in print. Oh joy! And some day, if you care passionately about making poems, you may publish a book, and books. Like Naphtali, you are a deer let loose, using a lifetime's worth of beautiful words.

Stanley Kunitz, a distinguished American poet in his nineties who won the Pulitzer Prize and was America's poet laureate, offers no illusions about the difficulties of the calling of poet. "Poetry," he says, "is the most difficult, the most solitary, and the most life-enhancing thing that one can do in the world."

12. Gathering of Poems

The poems in this section, some of which are mentioned in the text, are here for you to read and enjoy. They provide a good opportunity for you to put into practice the things you've learned about how poems work. Your teacher may have you analyze them for imagery, symbolism, irony, allusion, sound techniques, metrical structure, theme, tone, and so forth.

Storm Ending

Thunder blossoms gorgeously above our heads,
Great, hollow, bell-like flowers,
Rumbling in the wind,
Stretching clappers to strike our ears.
Full-lipped flowers
Bitten by the sun
Bleeding rain
Dripping rain like golden honey—
And the sweet earth flying from the thunder.

—Jean Toomer

The Tiger

Tiger! Tiger! burning bright
In the forests of the night,
What immortal hand or eye
Could frame thy fearful symmetry?

In what distant deeps or skies
Burnt the fire of thine eyes?
On what wings dare he aspire?
What the hand dare seize the fire?

And what shoulder, and what art,
Could twist the sinews of thy heart?
And when thy heart began to beat,
What dread hand forged thy dread feet?

What the hammer? what the chain?
In what furnace was thy brain?
What the anvil? what dread grasp
Dare its deadly terrors clasp?

When the stars threw down their spears,
And watered heaven with their tears,
Did he smile his work to see?
Did he who made the Lamb make thee?

Tiger! Tiger! burning bright
In the forests of the night,
What immortal hand or eye
Dare frame thy fearful symmetry?

—William Blake

Constantly risking absurdity

Constantly risking absurdity
and death
whenever he performs
above the heads
of his audience
the poet like an acrobat
climbs on rime
to a high wire of his own making
and balancing on eyebeams
above a sea of faces
paces his way
to the other side of day
performing entrechats
and sleight-of-foot tricks
and other high theatrics
and all without mistaking
any thing
for what it may not be
For he's the super realist
who must perforce perceive
taut truth
before the taking of each stance or step
in his supposed advance
toward that still higher perch
where Beauty stands and waits
with gravity
to start her death-defying leap
And he
a little charleychaplin man
who may or may not catch
her fair eternal form
spreadeagled in the empty air
of existence

—Lawrence Ferlinghetti

Traveling Through the Dark

Traveling through the dark I found a deer
dead on the edge of the Wilson River road.
It is usually best to roll them into the canyon:
the road is narrow; to swerve might make
  more dead.

By glow of the tail-light I stumbled back of the car
and stood by the heap, a doe, a recent killing;
she had stiffened already, almost cold.
I dragged her off; she was large in the belly.

My fingers touching her side brought me
  the reason—
her side was warm; her fawn lay there waiting,
alive, still, never to be born.
Beside that mountain road I hesitated.

The car aimed ahead its lowered parking lights;
under the hood purred the steady engine.
I stood in the glare of the warm exhaust turning red;
around our group I could hear the wilderness listen.

I thought hard for us all—my only swerving—
then pushed her over the edge into the river.

—William Stafford

Tantalus

If I end up in hell
condemned to what I am
it will be no clear well
nor the blood of the lamb
I crave; no sweet meadow

breeze; no bird-song casting
its lengthening shadow
to save me from wasting
blind in my own dry mask;
but a mountain, a stone
unequivocal task,
boulder and shoulder bone;
a rough work of the hands
and the tightening thighs,
the delight of commands—
that would be paradise.

—John Lynch

Saving Hands

My father never kissed me,
but he bloodied his hand once,
running it through an electric fan
to save mine. It left a scar.

My father never kissed me,
but he taught me how to hoe corn,
how to keep my fingers from cramping.
And he was happy.

My father never kissed me,
but he pulled from my hand a tenpenny nail
that had glanced from the hammer
while we were building a room.

I've kissed my son I have.
But I've never saved his hand.

—Sam Rasnake

Love

Love bade me welcome; yet my soul drew back
Guilty of dust and sin.
But quick-eyed Love, observing me grow slack
From my first entrance in,
Drew nearer to me, sweetly questioning
If I lack'd anything.
"A guest," I answered, "worthy to be here":
Love said, "You shall be he."
"I, the unkind, ungrateful? Ah, my dear,
I cannot look on Thee."
Love took my hand, and smiling did reply,
"Who made the eyes but I?"
"Truth, Lord; but I have marred them; let my shame
Go where it doth deserve."
"And know you not," says Love, "who bore
the blame?"
"My dear, then I will serve."
"You must sit down," says Love, "and taste
My meat."
So I did sit and eat.

—George Herbert

Trades

I want to be a carpenter,
To work all day long in clean wood,
Shaving it into little thin slivers
Which screw up into curls behind my plane;
Pounding square, black nails into white boards,
With the claws of my hammer glistening
Like the tongue of a snake.
I want to shingle a house,
Sitting on the ridgepole in a bright breeze.

I want to put the shingles on neatly,
Taking great care that each is directly between
two others.
I want my hands to have the tang of wood:
Spruce, cedar, cypress.
I want to draw a line on a board with a flat pencil,
And then saw along that line,
With the sweet-smelling sawdust piling up in a
yellow heap at my feet.
That is the life!
Heigh-ho!
It is much easier than to write this poem.

—Amy Lowell

Pied Beauty

Glory be to God for dappled things—
For skies of couple-color as a brinded[1] cow;
For rose-moles all in stipple upon trout that swim;
Fresh-firecoal chestnut-falls; finches' wings;
Landscape plotted and pieced—fold, fallow,
and plow;
And áll trádes, their gear and tackle and trim.[2]
All things counter, original, spare, strange;
Whatever is fickle, freckled (who knows how?)
With swift, slow; sweet, sour; adazzle, dim;
He fathers-forth whose beauty is past change:
Praise him.

—Gerard Manley Hopkins

[1] brinded: *streaked*
[2] trim: *equipment*

It Sifts From Leaden Sieves

It sifts from leaden sieves,
It powders all the wood.
It fills with alabaster wool
The wrinkles of the road.
It makes an even face
Of mountain and of plain—
Unbroken forehead from the east
Unto the east again.

It reaches to the fence,
It wraps it rail by rail
Till it is lost in fleeces;
It deals celestial veil

To stump and stack and stem—
A summer's empty room—
Acres of joints where harvests were,
Recordless,[3] but for them.

It ruffles wrists of posts
As ankles of a queen,
Then stills its artisans like ghosts,
Denying they have been.

—Emily Dickinson

Names of Horses

All winter your brute shoulders strained against
collars, padding
and steerhide over the ash hames, to haul
sledges of cordwood for drying through spring
and summer,

[3] recordless: *leaving no record*

for the Glenwood stove next winter, and for the
 simmering range.

In April you pulled cartloads of manure to spread on
 the fields,
dark manure of Holsteins, and knobs of your own
 clustered with oats.
All summer you mowed the grass in meadow and
 hayfield, the mowing machine
clacketing beside you, while the sun walked high in
 the morning;

and after noon's heat, you pulled a clawed rake
through the same acres,
gathering stacks, and dragged the wagon from stack
to stack,
and the built hayrack back, uphill to the chaffy barn,
three loads of hay a day from standing grass in the
 morning.
Sundays you trotted the two miles to church with
 the light load
of a leather quartertop buggy, and grazed in the
sound of hymns.
Generation on generation, your neck rubbed the
 windowsill
of the stall, smoothing the wood as the sea smooths
 glass.

When you were old and lame, when your shoulders
hurt bending to graze,
one October the man who fed you and kept you, and
 harnessed you every morning,
led you through corn stubble to sandy ground above
 Eagle Pond,
and dug a hole beside you where you stood
 shuddering in your skin,

and lay the shotgun's muzzle in the boneless hollow
behind your ear,
and fired the slug into your brain, and felled you
into your grave,
shoveling sand to cover you, setting goldenrod
upright above you,
where by next summer a dent in the ground made
your monument.
For a hundred and fifty years, in the pasture of
dead horses,
roots of pine trees pushed through the pale curves
of your ribs,
yellow blossoms flourished above you in autumn,
and in winter
frost heaved your bones in the ground—old toilers,
soil makers:
O Roger, Mackerel, Riley, Ned, Nellie, Chester,
Lady Ghost.

—Donald Hall

Tree, Tree

Tree, tree,
dry and green.

The girl of beautiful face
goes gathering olives.
The wind, that suitor of towers,
grasps her round the waist.
Four riders have passed
on Andalusian ponies,
with suits of azure and green,
and long dark cloaks.
"Come to Cordoba, lass."
The girl pays no heed.
Three young bullfighters have passed,
their waists are slender,

their suits orange-coloured,
their swords of antique silver.
"Come to Seville, lass."
The girl pays no heed.
When the evening became
purple, with diffused light,
a youth passed by bringing
roses and myrtles of the moon.
"Come to Granada, lass."
But the girl pays no heed.
The girl of beautiful face
still goes on gathering olives,
with the gray arm of the wind
encircling her waist.

—Federico Garciá Lorca

Death Be Not Proud

Death, be not proud, though some have called thee
Mighty and dreadful, for thou art not so;
For those whom you think'st thou dost overthrow
Die not, poor Death, nor yet canst thou kill me.
From rest and sleep, which but thy pictures be,
Much pleasure, then from thee much more must
flow,
And soonest our best men with thee do go,
Rest of their bones and souls' delivery.
Thou art slave to fate, chance, kings, and
desperate men,
And dost with poison, war, and sickness dwell,
And poppy, or charms can make us sleep as well,
And better than thy stroke; why swell'st thou then?
One short sleep past, we wake eternally,
And Death shall be no more; Death, thou shalt die.

—John Donne

Gethsemane

On a hill backlit by twilight,
the disciples gather like crows
for the night.

This is their down time, time to browse
among the olive branches, Christ with them,
their apostolic flight slowed at last to a
head-nodding drowse,
to a flutter of tattered cloak, the unraveling hem
dragging in the dirt like a hurt wing.
They flock momentarily around him,

then settle down, safe in the soft swing
of wind that rises and then falls back
with the deepening evening
into the distance, and sleep, while Christ's black
feathers burn in his father's fist,
plucked by God before by Judas kissed.

—Kelly Cherry

God's Grandeur

The world is charged with the grandeur of God.
It will flame out, like shining from shook foil;
It gathers to a greatness, like the ooze of oil
Crushed. Why do men then now not reck his rod?
Generations have trod, have trod, have trod;
And all is seared with trade; bleared, smeared
with toil;
And wears man's smudge and shares man's smell:
the soil
Is bare now, nor can foot feel, being shod.

And for all this, nature is never spent;
There lives the dearest freshness deep down things;

And though the last lights off the black West went
  Oh, morning, at the brown brink
    eastward, springs—
Because the Holy Ghost over the bent
  World broods with warm breast and with ah!
    bright wings.

—Gerard Manley Hopkins

Somewhere Along the Way

You lean on a wire fence, looking across
a field of grain with a man you have stopped
to ask for directions. You are not lost.
You stopped here only so you could take a moment
to see whatever this old farmer sees
who crumbles heads of wheat between his palms.
Rust is lifting the red paint from his barn roof,
and earth hardens over the sunken arc
of his mower's iron wheel. All his sons
have grown and moved away, and the old woman
keeps herself in the parlor where the light
is always too weak to make shadows. He sniffs

at the grain in his hand, and cocks an ear
toward a dry tree ringing with cicadas.
There are people dying today, he says,
that never died before. He lifts an arm
and points, saying what you already knew
about the way you are trying to go;
you nod and thank him, and think of going on,
but only after you have stood and listened
a little while longer to the soft click
of the swaying grain heads soon to be cut,
and the low voice, edged with dim prophecy,
that settles down around you like dust.

—Henry Taylor

Rinsed with Gold, Endless, Walking the Fields

Let this day's air praise the Lord–
Rinsed with gold, endless, walking the fields,
Blue and bearing the clouds like censers,
Holding the sun like a single note
Running through all things, a *basso profundo*
Rousing the birds to an endless chorus.
Let the river throw itself down before him,
The rapids laugh and flash with his praise,
Let the lake tremble about its edges
And gather itself in one clear thought
To mirror the heavens and the reckless gulls
That swoop and rise on its glittering shores.

Let the lawn burn continually before him
A green flame, and the tree's shadow
Sweep over it like the baton of a conductor,
Let winds hug the housecorners and woodsmoke
Sweeten the world with her invisible dress,
Let the cricket wind his heartspring
And draw the night by like a child's toy.

Let the tree stand and thoughtfully consider
His presence as its leaves dip and row
The long sea of wind, as sun and moon
Unfurl and decline like contending flags.
Let blackbirds quick as knives praise the Lord,
Let the sparrow line the moon for her nest
And pick the early sun for her cherry,
Let her slide on the outgoing breath of evening,
Telling of raven and dove,
The quick flutters, homings to the green houses.

Let the worm climb a winding stair,
Let the mole offer no sad explanation
As he paddles aside the dark from his nose,

Let the dog tug on the leash of his bark,
The startled cat electrically hiss,
And the snake sign her name in the dust

In joy. For it is he who underlies
The rock from its liquid foundation,
The sharp contraries of the giddy atom,
The unimaginable curve of space,
Time pulling like a patient string,
And gravity, fiercest of natural loves.

At his laughter, splendor riddles the night,
Galaxies swarm from a secret hive,
Mountains lift their heads from the sea,
Continents split and crawl for aeons
To huddle again, and planets melt
In the last tantrum of a dying star.

At his least signal spring shifts
Its green patina over half the earth,
Deserts whisper themselves over cities,
Polar caps widen and wither like flowers.

In his stillness rock shifts, root probes,
The spider tenses her geometrical ego,
The larva dreams in the heart of the peachwood,
The child's pencil makes a shaky line,
The dog sighs and settles deeper,
And a smile takes hold like the feet of a bird.

Sit straight, let the air ride down your backbone,
Let your lungs unfold like a field of roses,
Your eyes hang the sun and moon between them,
Your hands weigh the sky in even balance,
Your tongue, swiftest of members, release a word
Spoken at conception to the sanctum of genes,
And each breath rise sinuous with praise.

Let your feet move to the rhythm of your pulse
(Your joints like pearls and rubies he has hidden),
And your hands float high on the tide of your feelings.
Now, shout from the stomach, hoarse with music,
Give gladness and joy back to the Lord,
Who, sly as a milkweed, takes root in your heart.

—Robert Siegel

To His Coy Mistress

Had we but world enough and time,
This coyness,[4] lady, were no crime.
We would sit down and think which way
To walk, and pass our long love's day.
Thou by the Indian Ganges' side
Should'st rubies find; I by the tide
Of Humber would complain.[5] I would
Love you ten years before the Flood,
And you should, if you please, refuse
Till the conversion of the Jews.
My vegetable[6] love should grow
Vaster than empires, and more slow.
An hundred years should go to praise
Thine eyes, and on thy forehead gaze,
Two hundred to adore each breast,
But thirty thousand to the rest.
An age at least to every part,
And the last age should show your heart.
For, lady, you deserve this state,[7]
Nor would I love at lower rate.
    But at my back I always hear
Time's wingèd chariot hurrying near,

[4] coyness: *modesty, reluctance*
[5] complain: *sing sad songs*
[6] vegetable: *vegetative, flourishing*
[7] state: *pomp, ceremony*

And yonder all before us lie
Deserts of vast eternity.
Thy beauty shall no more be found,
Nor in thy marble vault shall sound
My echoing song; then worms shall try
That long preserved virginity,
And your quaint honor turn to dust,
And into ashes all my lust.
The grave's a fine and private place,
But none, I think, do there embrace.
    Now therefore, while the youthful hue
Sits on they skin like morning glew[8]
And while thy willing soul transpires
At every pore with instant[9] fires,
Now let us sport us while we may;
And now, like amorous birds of prey,
Rather at once our time devour
Than languish in his slow-chapped[10] power.
Let us roll all our strength and all
Our sweetness up into one ball
And tear our pleasures with rough strife
Thorough[11] the iron gates of life.
Thus, though we cannot make our sun
Stand still, yet we will make him run.

—Andrew Marvell

Birches

When I see birches bend to left and right
Across the lines of straighter darker trees,
I like to think some boy's been swinging them.
But swinging doesn't bend them down to stay

[8] glew: *glow*
[9] instant: *eager*
[10] slow-chapped: *slow-jawed*
[11] thorough: *through*

As ice-storms do. Often you must have seen them
Loaded with ice a sunny winter morning
After a rain. They click upon themselves
As the breeze rises, and turn many-colored
As the stir cracks and crazes their enamel.
Soon the sun's warmth makes them shed crystal
  shells
Shattering and avalanching on the snow-crust—
Such heaps of broken glass to sweep away
You'd think the inner dome of heaven had fallen.
They are dragged to the withered bracken by the load,
And they seem not to break; though once they
  are bowed
So low for long, they never right themselves:
You may see their trunks arching in the woods
Years afterwards, trailing their leaves on the ground
Like girls on hands and knees that throw their hair
Before them over their heads to dry in the sun.
But I was going to say when Truth broke in
With all her matter-of-fact about the ice-storm
I should prefer to have some boy bend them
As he went out and in to fetch the cows—
Some boy too far from town to learn baseball,
Whose only play was what he found himself,
Summer or winter, and could play alone.
One by one he subdued his father's trees
By riding them down over and over again
Until he took the stiffness out of them,
And not one but hung limp, not one was left
For him to conquer. He learned all there was
To learn about not launching out too soon
And so not carrying the tree away
Clear to the ground. He always kept his poise
To the top branches, climbing carefully
With the same pains you use to fill a cup
Up to the brim, and even above the brim.
Then he flung outward, feet first, with a swish,

Kicking his way down through the air to the ground.
So was I once myself a swinger of birches.
And so I dream of going back to be.
It's when I'm weary of considerations,
And life is too much like a pathless wood
Where your face burns and tickles with the cobwebs
Broken across it, and one eye is weeping
From a twig's having lashed across it open.
I'd like to get away from earth awhile
And then come back to it and begin over.
May no fate willfully misunderstand me
And half grant what I wish and snatch me away
Not to return. Earth's the right place for love:
I don't know where it's likely to go better.
I'd like to go by climbing a birch tree,
And climb black branches up a snow-white trunk
Toward heaven, till the tree could bear no more,
But dipped its top and set me down again.
That would be good both going and coming back.
One could do worse than be a swinger of birches.

—Robert Frost

Ulysses

It little profits that an idle king,
By this still hearth, among these barren crags,
Matched with an aged wife, I mete and dole
Unequal laws unto a savage race
That hoard, and sleep, and feed, and know not me.
I cannot rest from travel; I will drink
Life to the lees. All times I have enjoyed
Greatly, have suffered greatly, both with those
That loved me, and alone; on shore, and when
Through scudding drifts the rainy Hyades
Vexed the dim sea. I am become a name;
For always roaming with a hungry heart

Much have I seen and known—cities of men
And manners, climates, councils, governments,
Myself not least, but honored of them all—
And drunk delight of battle with my peers,
Far on the ringing plains of windy Troy.
I am a part of all that I have met;
Yet all experience is an arch wherethrough
Gleams that untraveled world whose margin fades
Forever and forever when I move.
How dull it is to pause, to make an end,
To rust unburnished, not to shine in use!
As though to breathe were life! Life piled on life
Were all too little, and of one to me
Little remains; but every hour is saved
From that eternal silence, something more,
A bringer of new things; and vile it were
For some three suns to store and hoard myself,
And this grey spirit yearning in desire
To follow knowledge like a sinking star,
Beyond the utmost bound of human thought.
   This is my son, mine own Telemachus,
To whom I leave the scepter and the isle—
Well-loved of me, discerning to fulfill
This labor, by slow prudence to make mild
A rugged people, and through soft degrees
Subdue them to the useful and the good.
Most blameless is he, centered in the sphere
Of common duties, decent not to fail
In offices of tenderness, and pay
Meet adoration to my household gods,
When I am gone. He works his work, I mine.
   There lies the port; the vessel puffs her sail;
There gloom the dark, broad seas. My mariners,
Souls that have toiled, and wrought, and thought
   with me—
That ever with a frolic welcome took

The thunder and the sunshine, and opposed
Free hearts, free foreheads—you and I are old;
Old age hath yet his honor and his toil.
Death closes all; but something ere the end,
Some work of noble note, may yet be done,
Not unbecoming men that strove with Gods.
The lights begin to twinkle from the rocks;
The long day wanes; the low moon climbs; the deep
Moans round with many voices. Come, my friends,
'Tis not too late to seek a newer world.
Push off, and sitting well in order smite
The sounding furrows; for my purpose holds
To sail beyond the sunset, and the baths
Of all the western stars, until I die.
It may be that the gulfs will wash us down;
It may be we shall touch the Happy Isles,
And see the great Achilles, whom we knew.
Though much is taken, much abides; and though
We are not now that strength which in old days
Moved earth and heaven, that which we are, we are—
One equal temper of heroic hearts,
Made weak by time and fate, but strong in will
To strive, to seek, to find, and not to yield.

—Alfred, Lord Tennyson

To Autumn

I

Season of mists and mellow fruitfulness,
  Close bosom-friend of the maturing sun;
Conspiring with him how to load and bless
  With fruit the vines that round the thatch-eaves run;
To bend with apples the mossed cottage-trees,
  And fill all fruit with ripeness to the core;
    To swell the gourd, and plump the hazel shells

With a sweet kernel; to set budding more,
And still more, later flowers for the bees,
Until they think warm days will never cease,
For Summer has o'er-brimmed their clammy cells.

II

Who hath not seen thee oft amid thy store?
Sometimes whoever seeks abroad may find
Thee sitting careless on a granary floor,
Thy hair soft-lifted by the winnowing wind;
Or on a half-reaped furrow sound asleep,
Drowsed with the fume of poppies, while thy hook
Spares the next swath and all its twinèd flowers:
And sometimes like a gleaner thou dost keep
Steady thy laden head across a brook;
Or by a cider-press, with patient look,
Thou watchest the last oozings hours by hours.

III

Where are the songs of Spring? Ay, where are they?
Think not of them, thou hast thy music too,—
While barred clouds bloom the soft-dying day,
And touch the stubble-plains with rosy hue;
Then in a wailful choir the small gnats mourn
Among the river sallows, borne aloft
Or sinking as the light wind lives or dies;
And full-grown lambs loud bleat from hilly bourn;
Hedge-crickets sing; and now with treble soft
The red-breast whistles from a garden-croft;
And gathering swallows twitter in the skies.

—John Keats

Here Follows Some Verses Upon the Burning of Our House—July 10th, 1666

Copied Out of a Loose Paper

In silent night when rest I took
For sorrow near I did not look
I wakened was with thund'ring noise
And piteous shrieks of dreadful voice.
That fearful sound of "Fire!" and "Fire!"
Let no man know is my desire.
I, starting up, the light did spy,
And to my God my heart did cry
To strengthen me in my distress
And not to leave me succorless.
Then, coming out, beheld a space
The flame consume my dwelling place.
And when I could no longer look,
I blest His name that gave and took,
That laid my goods now in the dust.
Yea, so it was, and so 'twas just.
It was His own, it was not mine,
Far be it that I should repine;
He might of all justly bereft
But yet sufficient for us left.
When by the ruins oft I past[12]
My sorrowing eyes aside did cast,
And here and there the places spy
Where oft I sat and long did lie:
Here stood that trunk, and there that chest,
There lay that store I counted best.
My pleasant things in ashes lie
And them behold no more shall I.
Under thy roof no guest shall sit,
Nor at thy table eat a bit.

[12] past: *passed*

No pleasant tale shall e'er be told.
Nor things recounted done of old.
No candle e'er shall shine in thee,
Nor bridegroom's voice e'er heard shall be.
In silence ever shall thou lie,
Adieu, Adieu, all's vanity.
Then straight I 'gin my heart to chide,
And did thy wealth on earth abide?
Didst fix thy hope on mold'ring dust?
The arm of flesh didst make thy trust?
Raise up thy thoughts above the sky
That dunghill mists away may fly.
Thou hast an house on high erect,
Framed by that mighty Architect,
With glory richly furnished,
Stands permanent though this be fled.
It's purchased and paid for too
By Him who hath enough to do.
A price so vast as is unknown
Yet by His gift is made thing own;
There's wealth enough, I need no more,
Farewell, my pelf,[13] farewell my store.
The world no longer let me love,
My hope and treasure lies above.

—Anne Bradstreet

Questioning Faces

The winter owl banked just in time to pass
And save herself from breaking window glass.
And her wings straining suddenly aspread

[13] pelf: *possessons, usually with the implication they are gained by questionable means.*

Caught color from the last of evening red
In a display of underdown and quill
To glassed-in children at the window sill.

—Robert Frost

The Joys of House Wrecking

Builders are a sorry lot. They start low,
they follow rules. Wreckers stop at the top,
unroofing under the sun, releasing prisoner
nails to the society of grass below,
flying frisbee shingles some drudge lugged up
to random lodging in the kudzu's throat.

Like those ten-year-old surgeons, rubber-gloved
and skittish behind the shadowing sheet,
who lift to the joy of the summer-camp crowd
all manner of junk from the patient's gullet
or gut-sausages, a mop, old swords, or a large fish—
I strip away sheathing and haul from the attic
all unretrieved shards, hulks, husks,
the comic bones of incompetent beds, raggedy rags,
a grey mattress brain with a low I.Q.
All turn in the air. All fall down.
Gravity plays my game.
Now ceiling bone connected to de. . .
wall bone, wall bone connected de. . .
floor bone, now hear de word of de. . .
Wrecking bar. It talks loud,
it talks the house down
in a hurry of plaster and soot.

Liberate that lath! Hoist a joist!
Free that window—he's been framed!

In my joy under the sun,
I follow the head of my eight-pound sledge,
I follow no rule but the rule of break,
bury the bits in the cellar,
turn back time to a zero house.
I sing in the sun and wonder
how the Big Wrecker can wait.

—Larry Richman

Mummy Slept Late and Daddy Fixed Breakfast

Daddy fixed breakfast.
He made us each a waffle.
It looked like gravel pudding.
It tasted something awful.

"Ha, ha," he said, "I'll try again.
This time I'll get it right."
But what *I* got was in between
Bituminous and anthracite.

"A little too well done? Oh well,
I'll have to start all over."
That time what landed on my plate
Looked like a manhole cover.
I tried to cut it with a fork:
The fork gave off a spark.
I tried a knife and twisted it
Into a question mark.

I tried it with a hack-saw.
I tried it with a torch.
It didn't even make a dent.
It didn't even scorch.

The next time Dad gets breakfast
When Mummy's sleeping late,
I think I'll skip the waffles.
I'd sooner eat the plate!

—John Ciardi

Sonnet 73

That time of year thou mayst in me behold
When yellow leaves, or none, or few, do hang
Upon those boughs which shake against the cold,
Bare ruined choirs where late the sweet birds sang.
In me thou see'st the twilight of such day
As after sunset fadeth in the west,
Which by-and-by black night doth take away,
Death's second self that seals up all in rest.
In me thou see'st the glowing of such fire
That on the ashes of his youth doth lie,
As the deathbed where on it must expire,
Consumed with that which it was nourished by.
This thou perceiv'st, which makes thy love
more strong,
To love that well which thou must leave ere long.

—William Shakespeare

Root Cellar

Nothing would sleep in that cellar, dank as a ditch,
Bulbs broke out of boxes hunting for chinks in
the dark,
Shoots dangled and drooped,
Lolling obscenely from mildewed crates,
Hung down long yellow evil necks, like
tropical snakes.

And what a congress of stinks!—
Roots ripe as old bait,
Pulpy stems, rank, silo-rich,
Leaf-mold, manure, lime, piled against
  slippery planks.
Nothing would give up life:
Even the dirt kept breathing a small breath.

—Theodore Roethke

The Wood, The Weed, The Wag

Three things there be that prosper all apace
And flourish while they grow asunder far;
But on a day, they meet all in a place,
And when they meet, they one another mar.

And they be these: the wood, the weed, the wag.
The wood is that which makes the gallows tree;
The weed is that which strings the hangman's bag;
The wag, my pretty knave, betokens thee.

Now mark, dear boy, while these assemble not,
Green springs the tree, hemp grows, the wag is wild.
But when they meet, it makes the timber rot,
It frets the halter, and it chokes the child.

—Sir Walter Raleigh
(To his son)

Teacher's Annex

Besides the exercises and writing activities mentioned in the book, the following are offered to promote creative thinking. The mind is led to move beyond conventional categories and freely pursue associations. I've used all these exercises with good success.

1. Oona and Kepik. This is adapted from Stephen Minot's book *Three Genres*.

Draw two shapes on the board:

Say to students, if one is Oona and one is Kepik, tell which is which.

One is male and the other female.
One is oil and one is gasoline.
One is a drum and one is a violin.

One is the wind, the other a dog's bark.
One is a lemon, the other a melon.
One is a saxophone and one is a trumpet.

Most all audiences give the same responses, with Oona being female and flowy, and Kepik male and sharp. These associations have their own kind of logic, with one sense spilling over into another. The word for this is synesthesia, as when one says a color is "loud." Here are some further activities using Oona and Kepik.

» Go through the dictionary and find fifty words that are distinctly Oona or Kepik. For example, "swoon," "bleed," and "snowy" are Oona words. "Guzzle," "jagged," and "kickbox" are more Kepik-like. Type the words in columns (double-spaced) and have students go through the list, writing O for Oona and K for Kepik. Some disagreement is to be expected. Kids enjoy this.

» Imagine either a Kepik or Oona place, and write a paragraph or poem describing it. The idea is to think of a landscape and words that match Kepik or Oona, as in the following example:

The desert is a kepik place. The sand is scorching and gritty. The sun blazes down on my parched cheeks. Plants are thick and scrubby. I touch the needles of a cactus and feel a quick sting. In the distance, jagged mountains scrape the sky. The sudden screech of a hawk shatters the silence. I am tortured with thoughts of water, for a fire burns in my throat and I have far to go.

2. Nature Study. Collect several natural objects: a conch shell, a hiking stick, a pine cone, a coconut, a hawk or goose feather, a leaf, a rock. (Sometimes I include a clear glass marble.) Distribute the objects. Have each student study the object, then make a list of at least fifteen descriptive details involving the senses. Next, have students think of at least two metaphors/similes which come to mind. (*Example:* Brown leaf reminds me of an old person's hand.) Finally, ask students to tell some ways in which *they* are like the object and to write a poem based on these comparisons.

3. Silly Simile. This game comes from *The Magic Pencil* by Eve Shelnutt and is popular with all ages. Hand out three index cards (3 x 5") to students. Also give them colored markers. Ask them to write a noun on one of the cards and another noun on a second card. Collect the noun cards. Have them write an action verb on the third card. Collect the verb cards. Make one card that says LIKE. On a long table, place face-down the first set of noun cards. Beside these place the other noun cards. Beside these place the verb cards face down. Face up place the LIKE card. To the right of this, place the other noun cards face down. Have the students take turns flipping the cards over to reveal the similes. "The pig crawled like a jelly bean." "A door wiggled like a vitamin." (You can have the students add articles to precede the nouns as they read their sentences.) The results are always unexpected and hilarious. Sometimes they even make sense (sort of!).

4. Fishy Words. Have students read Elizabeth Bishop's poem "The Fish" on page 122. Discuss it. Then place old newspapers on each desk or table. Have everyone close his or her eyes. Place a raw fish in front of each student (your local fish market can give you these or sell them cheap, especially if you mention it's for educational purposes). Now tell them to write a fish poem. The deadness of the fish, the beauty of its coloration, its scales and other features (including the smell!) seem to evoke strong reactions and lead to wonderful poems.

5. Wild Thing. This assignment is adapted from Kenneth Koch's popular book *Rose, Where Did You Get That Red?* Have students read William Blake's "Tiger, Tiger." Discuss the poem, especially the wildness and mystery of the tiger. Now have students observe an animal (not a pet): a chicken, a salamander, a snake, etc., and write a poem exploring the animal's mystery. (They could observe via a television program if they wish.) They might want to write an apostrophe to the animal, posing a series of questions or a single question: Fish, where did you get those eyes of coin?

6. Hats Off. This activity enables students to capture the essence of personality through a simple prop. Ask students to bring an unusual hat to class. It can be funny, crazy, or sophisticated. It might be one that belonged to a grandparent or a little brother. Then have them develop a character based on the hat and write a poem that shows his or her personality (especially quirks!). The following poem can be used to illustrate. I wore to class an old-fashioned hat of blue and green fabric feathers with a veil. It may help for the writer to pose a question, as in the example.

Forgetful Mrs. Merriwether

Mrs. Thelma Merriwether,
why don't you look up?
Hastening with mouse-quick steps
to market, blue feathered hat
dipping and tipping as you hurry along
the sidewalk, your sturdy black shoes
leading like seeing-eye shoes, your mind
filling its drawers labeled Meats and Fruits
and a special drawer for the caraway seed
you musn't forget this time
since you promised Mrs. Trickle a loaf
of your very best rye, or was it cracked
wheat she requested? Oh dear, you'll need

molasses, too. And a catnip ball for Pumpkin
who sleeps in a curve at your feet, but wait,
where is that Pumpkin? She hasn't touched
her food for days . . . or weeks.
And why didn't you bring your umbrella?
It's starting to rain a cold, stinging rain.
If only you'd looked up,
you would have known.

7. Collaborative Holiday Poem. This exercise works well with a group of eight or more students. I've used it for Christmas and Easter, but it can also be composed after a nature walk. It helps students develop metaphors and use concrete language. Get ready for surprises! For this, you will need one large poster board, tape or glue, colored markers, and poster board cut in long strips and measuring about an inch or so in height.

Pass out a basket with folded papers on which appear words representing aspects of the Nativity: Holy Child, Mary, Magi, manger, oxen, the road to Bethlehem, the donkey, Joseph, doves, etc. Each student chooses one paper. Have each person compose a line beginning with "I sing of . . ." in which they elaborate on the image written on their paper. They must use concrete or metaphorical language. After you have approved their lines, have them print each line neatly on a strip of posterboard using a colored marker.

Example: I sing of an ox, nuzzling a Savior's head
in the sleepy dark of a stable.

When everyone is finished, lay the strips on the large board. Have one or all students decide on the proper order of lines. Once eveyone is agreed, tape the lines on the board. Leave room for the title (we called ours "Nativity Song: A Collaborative Christmas Poem"). Read the poem aloud. Later, type up the poem and make copies for the class with the authors' names appearing at the end. This makes a lovely gift to include with Christmas cards.

As a variation, you can also give out objects associated with Christmas (or some other holiday): bell, candy cane, candle, sprig of holly, pine cone, basket, etc. Then pass the hat with folded papers on which are written different attributes of God. Have each student write a line of poetry bringing into association the attribute and the object through a simile or metaphor. Each line begins with the attribute, followed by the simile: "God's holiness is like a pure white snowflake." "Jesus' glory is like a basket, simple and strong."

8. Poetry Performance. Have students read and memorize a poem such as Nancy Willard's "The Cat to His Dinner" (page 81) or Shakespeare's "All the World's a Stage" from *As You Like It*, or one of Ogden Nash's humorous poems. Have them interpret and enact the poem for an audience using gestures, vocal expression, bodily movement, masks, etc.

Glossary

accented syllable—syllable that receives an emphasis of sound, contributing to the rhythm of a line of verse. In scanning a poem, accented syllables are denoted with (´).

accentual meter—a kind of meter dating back to Old English made up of lines having the same number of accented syllables. In Old English, every line had four, but the pattern has been modified to allow the poet to set the number of accents. These may appear anywhere in the line and include any number of unaccented syllables.

allegory—a narrative (story) told in the form of poetry or prose in which the events and characters remind the reader of other known meanings. These meanings can be historical, moral, religious or political. A new story is told as a way of telling an old story. *Pilgrim's Progress* is the most famous allegory.

alliteration—repetition of initial consonant sounds as in "The force that through the green fuse drives the flower" (*f* sounds).

allusions—references in literature to famous historical or religious events, or to other works of literature.

antithetic parallelism—a Hebrew "thought rhyme" of two opposite ideas expressed in parallel lines.

apostrophe—a figure of speech wherein the speaker of the poem directly addresses, or speaks to an absent person, an inanimate thing, or an abstraction such as love or death: "Time, why do you punish me?" "O Death, where is thy victory?"

approximate rhyme (also called **slant rhyme**)—words in proximity having similar but inexact correspondence of sound as in "never/waiver," "tall/tale," and "bean/heat." Sometimes the ending sounds will be the same; sometimes the internal sounds will correspond.

assonance—when vowel sounds of neighboring words are the same: "shook/wood," "meek/green." (Notice that these are also approximate rhymes.)

aubade—a morning love song.

ballad—a story in verse that is sung.

blank verse—unrhymed lines of iambic pentameter. Shakespeare's plays are written largely in blank verse; likewise Milton's *Paradise Lost.*

cacophony—jarring, inharmonious sounds.

caesura—a pause within a line of poetry.

climactic parallelism—Hebrew poetic form of paired lines in which the second line repeats and builds on the idea stated in the first.

closed couplet—two rhymed lines of iambic pentameter. Also known as the **heroic couplet**, the closed couplet expresses a complete thought.

closed form—a literary form such as the sonnet, handed down through generations, which follows established conventions. Also known as **received** and **fixed form.**

connotation—emotional weight carried by words. A word's connotation goes beyond the literal meaning. "Skinny" and "slim" both mean "thin," but the first is what S.I. Hiakawa calls a "snarl" word and the other, a "purr" word.

consonance—sound effect achieved in poetry when neighboring words end in the same consonant, as in "time" and "team."

cosmic irony—see **irony of situation**.

couplet—paired lines of poetry with similar end rhymes.

denotation—the literal or dictionary meaning of a word.

diction—the word choices used by a writer to convey a given effect. In an ironic poem about the experience of inner city black youths, Gwendolyn Brooks writes, "We real cool. We/left school..." Here, the diction is that of the street. Compare with the formal tone of the speaker in in T. S. Eliot's famous poem, "The Love Song of J. Alfred Prufrock": "Let us go then, you and I/When the evening is spread out against the sky."

didactic poetry—poetry that teaches a moral lesson.

dramatic irony—a discrepancy between what the reader knows and what a character or the speaker of a poem knows.

dramatic monologue—poem presented as a speech by a character at a dramatic moment in his or her life. The character is speaking to another party who remains silent. Robert Browning is the master of this type.

elegy—a poem written as a reflection on death or a serious theme. Elegies are often composed to commemorate the death of a particular individual. Traditionally, they follow a set meter called the elegiac (one verse of dactylic hexameter followed by one of pentameter).

end rhyme—rhyme occuring with the last word of a line.

end-stopped line—a line of poetry that achieves grammatical completion at the end of the line.

English sonnet—also called the **Shakespearean sonnet**, this kind of poem has fourteen lines that follow a fixed pattern of rhyme: *abab cdcd efef gg.*

enjambment—poetic device of carrying the sense of one line over into the next through means of a run-on line.

envoy—a short, fixed, final stanza of certain poems.

epic—a long narrative poem chronicling the adventures of national heroes. The *Odyssey* and the *Iliad* are examples.

epigram—a short poem, often satiric, that considers a single thought or occurrence and includes a clever turn of thought: "Man proposes but God disposes."

euphony—pleasing, harmonious sounds.

exact rhyme—words in close proximity having different initial sounds but the same vowel and consonant sounds as in "damp/tramp" and "hummer/drummer."

figurative language—language that is meant to be taken imaginatively and not literally.

figures of speech—imaginative devices used to gain surprise and freshness of speech, to create word pictures, and to show similarities in things normally not associated together. Metaphor, simile, symbolism, paradox, hyperbole, understatement, apostrophe, personification, irony, and metonymy are some of the well-known figures of speech.

fixed form—see **closed form, received form.**

foot—basic rhythmic unit of metrical poetry. The feet have various names: iamb, trochee, anapest, dactyl, and spondee.

free form—also known as **open form.** The poet follows no prescribed metrical pattern but allows the words and lines to create the form. White space and sound devices are often utilized imaginatively.

free verse—poetry that avoids regular rhymes and meters but uses rhythmic effects, as with the Song of Solomon and Walt Whitman's "Song of Myself." It was the major verse form of the twentieth century.

haiku—traditional Japanese poem consisting of three lines following the pattern of five, seven, five syllables per line and offering a flash of insight.

heroic couplet—also known as the **closed couplet.** Composed of two rhymed lines of iambic pentameter.

hyperbole—a figure of speech in which exaggeration, or **overstatement**, is employed for effect. More truth is given to convey truth.

imagery—words appealing to the senses of sight, sound, touch, taste, and smell.

internal rhyme—rhyme occurring within a line rather than at the end.

irony—a gap or incongruity between expectation and reality, between appearance and substance, between reader and character or between characters.

irony of situation—a twist of fate in which the outcome one expects is thwarted and another outcome, disappointing or terrible, occurs. Also known as **cosmic irony.**

Italian sonnet—also called the **Petrarchan sonnet**, after the fourteenth-century Italian poet Petrarch. It is composed of fourteen lines grouped into the octave (first eight lines) and sestet (last six lines). This sonnet follows the rhyme scheme *abbaabba cdcdcd* (or *cde cde*).

lyric—a short poem expressing imagination and feeling, presented from the viewpoint of a single speaker. The lyric originally came from ancient Greek drama to describe an actor who stepped forward to sing a song to the accompaniment of a lyre.

metaphor—a comparison between two unlike things that uses no connecting words such as "like" or "as." Sometimes the word metaphor is used to include simile, as well.

metaphorming—the art of finding similarity between dissimilar things; in other words, making **metaphors**.

meter—the deliberate and recurrent use of accents and pauses in a line of poetry.

metonymy—a figure of speech in which a part of something is used to represent the whole, or something closely associated with an object or idea is used to represent it. "Daily bread" in the Lord's Prayer represents all the food we eat each day.

narrative poem—a poem that tells a story.

octave—the first eight lines of an **Italian sonnet** which form a unit of thought posed as an issue or problem to be resolved in the sestet.

onomatopoeia—words that snap, crackle, and pop; in other words, sound like that which they represent.

open couplet—a couplet in which the thought expressed is not complete but carried over into the next couplet.

open form—see **free form**.

overstatement—see **hyperbole**.

pantoum—a Malaysian form of revolving rhymes divided into **quatrains**. The pantoum repeats the second and fourth lines of one stanza as the first and third lines of the next.

The rhyme scheme is *abab, abab.* In the final quatrain, the first and third lines of the first stanza are repeated in reverse order, so that the poem ends with its opening line.

parable—a story, usually allegorical, designed to teach moral truth.

paradox—a figure of speech which presents an apparent, but not actual, contradiction.

parallelism—lines that correspond in thought and structure by giving equal weight to both. Hebrew poetry is based on this device.

pastoral—a poem about shepherds and country life. It comes from the Latin word for shepherd, *pastor.* Today the term is used to include poems about rural life and people.

personae—fictitious speaker of a poem (not to be confused with the author of the poem).

personification—a figure of speech in which a thing, an animal, or an idea is given human qualities.

Petrarchan sonnet—see **Italian sonnet.**

poetic diction—the use of archaic expressions such as "n'er" and "o'er" that "sound" poetic but are really cardboard words borrowed mostly from the Romantic era. Wannabe poets and those who don't bother to read contemporary poetry are often guilty of using this kind of diction.

prosody—the art of scanning a line in a poem, which is to say, of analyzing its metrical pattern.

quatrain—four-line stanzas that in English poetry are the most common.

received form—see **closed form, fixed form.**

simile—a comparison between two unlike things that uses the words "like" or "as" to make the comparison.

rhyme—matching sounds among words in a poem, sometimes exact and sometimes approximate.

rhyme royal—a stanza of seven lines written in iambic pentameter following the rhyme scheme *ababbcc.*

rhythm—the recurrence of accented and unaccented syllables.

romance—a literary work which "describes what never happened nor is likely to happen," according to Clara Reeve, and which presents heroic deeds and grand adventures.

scan—to describe the metrical structure of a poem in order to better understand its meaning.

sestina—a complex Italian form from medieval times that means "song of sixes" because it is composed of six six-line stanzas with six end-words repeated in a fixed order throughout the poem.

sestet—the final six lines in an **Italian sonnet** which together present a resolution or finale to an issue or problem posed in the octave.

Shakespearean sonnet—see **English sonnet.**

simile—a comparison between two unlike things that uses the words like or as to make the comparison.

slack syllable—syllable in a word that receives little emphasis in relation to the accented syllable of the same word. Also called unaccented or unstressed syllable.

slant rhyme—see **approximate rhyme.**

soliloquy—a speech given by a character in a play which is intended to represent his or her thoughts as if spoken aloud and alone, heard only by the audience, though other characters may be present on stage.

Spenserian stanza—a nine-line stanza. The first eight lines are written in iambic pentameter.

stanza—group of lines that follows a metrical pattern repeated throughout the poem.

stressed syllable—see **accented syllable.**

syllabic verse—a verse pattern in which the number of syllables per line is fixed by tradition, as in **haiku**, or determined by the poet, as in Dylan Thomas's "Fern Hill."

symbol—an image given prominence in a literary work and which suggests multiple meanings.

synonymous parallelism—in Hebrew poetry, the presentation of an idea in one line which is said differently in the second parallel line.

style—the manner in which a writer expresses himself in order to convey his ideas and purposes. The language used by the author reflects his individuality, becoming a kind of recognizable signature.

tercet—a stanza of three lines, also called a **triplet.**

terza rima—a poem written in tercets using an interlocking rhyme scheme of *aba, bcb, cdc, ded*, and so on. This is the pattern used by Dante in *The Divine Comedy.*

tone—the attitude toward subject and audience conveyed in a work of literature.

triplet—see **tercet.**

understatement—a figure of speech in which less is said to say more. Restraint and sometimes sarcasm characterize understatement.

unstressed syllable—see **slack syllable.**

verbal irony—a form of irony in which the words spoken mean the opposite of what they appear to say.

verisimilitude—the appearance of being true and actual.

verse—metrical language.

villanelle—a French received form made of **tercets**, typically five, and a closing **quatrain.** It uses a complex, interlocking rhyme scheme that goes like this: the first and third lines of the first tercet are alternately repeated as the final lines of the tercets which follow. These lines reappear as a couplet in the quatrain.

Author/Poet Index

Poem Index

Y

Acknowledgments

The author wishes to thank the following students for granting permission to include their poems in this book: Rachael Emery, Chris Greene, Jeannie Imbody, Rachel LeBeau, Hannah Lepsch, Candace Johnson, Joshua Rutledge, William Caleb Rutledge, and Emily Windes.

"Any Morning" by William Stafford, copyright by William Stafford. Originally published in *Ohio Review*, 1993. Reprinted by permission of The Estate of William Stafford.

"Apple Count" by Robert Morgan. Reprinted by permission of Robert Morgan.

"The Cat to His Dinner" by Nancy Willard, from *Water Walker*, copyright © 1989 by Nancy Willard. Reprinted by permission of Alfred A. Knopf, a Division of Random House, Inc.; Copyright for non-exclusive English language rights throughout the British Commonwealth by Naggar Agency.

"Constantly risking absurdity" by Lawrence Ferlinghetti, from *A Coney Island of the Mind*, copyright © 1958 by Lawrence Ferlinghetti. Reprinted by permission of New Directions Publishing Corp.

"The Fish" by Elizabeth Bishop, from *The Complete Poems: 1927-1979*, copyright © 1971, 1983 by Alice Helen Methfessel. Reprinted by permission of Farrar, Straus and Giroux, LLC.

"Gethsemane" by Kelly Cherry, from *God's Loud Hand*. Reprinted by permission of LSU Press. Copyright © 1993. Permission granted does not include matter within the material to be used for which LSU Press does not own the rights.

"Golden Delicious" by Luci Shaw, from *Writing the River*, copyright © 1994 by Luci Shaw. Reprinted by permission of Luci Shaw.

Haiku by David Oates, from *Shifting with my Sandwich Hand: Haiku, Senryu and Such*. Published by Monkey Books, Athens, GA, 1999. Reprinted by permission of David Oates.

"The Hand That Signed the Paper," "Fern Hill," "Do Not Go Gentle Into That Good Night" by Dylan Thomas, from *The Poems of Dylan Thomas*, copyright © 1952 by Dylan Thomas. Reprinted by permission of New Directions Publishing Corp. ; for world rights excluding the USA, reprinted by permission of David Higham Associates Limited.

"He Wishes for the Cloths of Heaven" by W. B. Yeats from *The Collected Poems of W. B. Yeats,* Revised Second Edition, edited by Richard J. Finneran, copyright © 1983, 1989 by Anne Yeats. Reprinted with permission of Scribner, a Division of Simon and Schuster; for rights throughout the British Commonwealth, reprinted with permission of A.P. Watts Limited on behalf of Michael B. Yeats.

"Heritage" by James Still, from *A Southern Appalachian Reader,* copyright © 1989 by James Still. Reprinted by permission of Appalachian Consortium Press.

"The Joys of House Wrecking" by Larry Richman. Reprinted by permission of Larry Richman.

"Keeper of the Vines" by Rebecca B. Morecraft, from *Roots and Vines*, copyright © 1999 by Rebecca B. Morecraft. Reprinted by permission of Rebecca B. Morecraft.

"The Lake Isle of Innisfree" by W.B. Yeats, from *The Collected Poems of W.B. Yeats*, copyright © 1938 by Simon and Schuster Trade. Reprinted by permission of Simon and Schuster Trade.

"Mummy Slept Late and Daddy Fixed Breakfast" by John Ciardi, copyright © 1962 by John Ciardi. Reprinted by permission of HarperCollins Publishers. This selection may not be re-illustrated.

"My Grandmother Washes Her Vessels" by Fred Chappell, from *River*, copyright © 1975 by Fred Chappell. Reprinted by permission of Louisiana State University Press.

"My Mother Smites the Sun" by Suzanne Clark, from *What a Light Thing, This Stone*, copyright © 1999 by Suzanne Clark.

"My Papa's Waltz," by Theodore Roethke, from *Collected Poems of Theodore Roethke* by Theodore Roethke, copyright © 1942 by

Hearst Magazines, Inc. Reprinted by permission of Doubleday, a division of Random House, Inc.

"Names of Horses" by Donald Hall, from *Old and New Poems*, copyright © 1990 by Donald Hall. Reprinted by permission of Houghton Mifflin Company. All rights reserved. Originally published in *The New Yorker.*

"Oona and Kepik" by Stephen Minot. Reprinted by permission of Stephen Minot.

"Paysage Moralise" ("Hearing of Harvests Rotting in the Valleys") by W. H. Auden, from *W. H. Auden Collected Poems*, copyright © 1937 and renewed 1965 by W. H. Auden. Reprinted by permission of Random House, Inc. Reprinted by permission of Faber and Faber Limited for non-exclusive English language rights in British Commonwealth.

"Rinsed with Gold, Endlessly, Walking the Fields" by Robert Siegel, from *In a Pig's Eye*, copyright © 1980 by Robert Siegel. Reprinted by permission of Robert Siegel.

"Shelter" by Bruce Wiegl, from *The American Poetry Review,* March/April 1992, copyright by Bruce Weigl. Reprinted by permission of Bruce Weigl.

"Silly Similie" by Eve Shelnutt, from *The Magic Pencil* by Eve Shelnutt. Copyright © 1994. Used by permission of Peachtree Publishers, LTD.

"Snow in Spring" by Ivy O. Eastwick from, *I Rode the Black Horse Far Away*, copyright © 1960 by Ivy O. Eastwick. Used by permission of Abingdon Press.

"Somewhere Along the Way" by Henry Taylor, from *The Flying Change*, copyright © 1985 by Henry Taylor. Reprinted by permission of Louisiana State University Press.

"Song for Wood's Barbecue Shack" by Jeff Daniel Marion, from *Lost and Found*, copyright © 1994 by Jeff Daniel Marion. Reprinted by permission of The Sow's Ear Press.

"Stopping by the Woods on a Snowy Evening" and "Questioning Faces" by Robert Frost from *The Poetry of Robert Frost* edited by Edward Connery Lathem, copyright © 1923, copyright 1969 by Henry Holt and Co., copyright © 1951, 1962 by Robert Frost. Reprinted by permission of Henry Holt and Company, LLC.

"Storm Ending," from *Cane* by Jean Toomer. Copyright © 1923 by Boni & Liveright, renewed 1951 by Jean Toomer. Used by permission of Liveright Publishing Corporation.

"Transfigured Bird" by James Merrill, from *Selected Poems 1946-1985* by James Merrill, copyright © 1992 by James Merrill. Reprinted by permission of Alfred A. Knopf, a Division of Random House Inc.

"Traveling through the Dark" by William Stafford copyright © 1962, 1998 by the Estate of William Stafford. Reprinted from *The Way It Is: New & Selected Poems* with the permission of Graywolf Press, Saint Paul Minnesota.

"Tree, Tree" by Frederico Garcia Lorca, translated by Stephen Spender and J. L. Gili, from *The Selected Poems of Federico Garcia Lorca,* copyright © 1955 by New Directions Publishing Corp. Reprinted by permission of New Directions Publishing Corp; copyright for British Commonwealth by David Higham Associates, Limited

"To An Athlete Dying Young" and "Is My Team Ploughing" from *The Collected Poems of A. E. Housman*, copyright © 1965 by Henry Holt and Co. Permission granted by Society of Authors as the literary representative of the Estate of A.E. Housman.

"Wild Thing" by Kenneth Koch, from *Rose, Where Did You Get That Red?* copyright 1973 by Kenneth Koch. Reprinted by permission of Random House, Inc. Reprinted in the British Commonwealth by permission of International Creative Management, Inc. Copyright © 1973 by Kenneth Koch.

"The Writer" by Richard Wilbur, from *The Mind Reader*, copyright © 1971 by Richard Wilbur. Reprinted by permission of Harcourt, Inc. Reprinted by permission of Faber and Faber, Ltd. for non-exclusive English language rights throughout the British Commonwealth.